DECADE OF THE TRAINS
the 1940s

DECADE OF THE TRAINS

the 1940s

Photoessay and Commentary by
DON BALL, JR.

Text by
ROGERS E. M. WHITAKER
("E. M. Frimbo")

NEW YORK GRAPHIC SOCIETY
BOSTON

Back shop (DELANO)

To Whitney

Don Ball, Jr.

Photoessay and Commentary Copyright © 1977 by Don Ball, Jr.
Text Copyright © 1977 by Rogers E. M. Whitaker

First Edition, 1977
First Paperback Edition, 1980
Third Paperback Printing, 1987

LIBRARY OF CONGRESS CATALOGING IN PUBLICATION DATA

Ball, Don, Jr.
    Decade of the trains.

    1.   Railroads—United States—History. 2.   United
States—Description and travel—1940-1960.
I.   Whitaker, Rogers E. M., joint author. II.   Title.
TF23.B334 1977   385′.3′0973   77-12593
ISBN 0-8212-0759-8

Designed by Bernard Schleifer

New York Graphic Society books are published by Little,
Brown and Company.
Published simultaneously in Canada by Little, Brown &
Company (Canada) Limited.

Printed in the United States of America

CONTENTS

PHOTO CREDITS

Credits are listed in captions in the following sequence: left-hand page, top to bottom; right-hand page, top to bottom. Where all photographs on a page or spread are by the same person, only one name appears. Photographs by Don Ball, Jr., are indicated as BALL; negatives in his collection are credited as COLLECTION, and unidentified prints in his collection as PRINT COLLECTION. Negatives in the Howard Fogg and Bill Wolfer collections are designated similarly. The author is grateful to those railroads that have supplied photographs from their archives, to the Library of Congress for the use of Office of War Information photographs, and to the photographers:

J. S. Bennett	Charles H. Kerrigan
Kent W. Cochrane	James G. LaVake
Robert L. Collins	Robert G. Lewis
Richard J. Cook	Ed Nowak
Jack Delano	Al Palmer
T. J. Donahue	John Pickett
Howard Fogg	Roger S. Plummer
James P. Gallagher	Phil Ronfor
Henry R. Griffiths, Jr.	John Vachon
Philip R. Hastings	Marion Post Wolcott
Harley Kelso	J. J. Young

San Augustine, Texas, waiting room, April 1943. (VACHON)

A PAGE FROM THE DIARY OF DON BALL, SR.

Sunday, December 7, 1941

We are at war with Japan! This news was first given me by
Ginny at 4:30 when Mary and I drove in to have supper with her. It
stunned me. At dawn today Jap bombers blasted our Naval, Army
and Air centers in Hawaii and the Philippines; it was an attack of
unmitigated treachery, deliberately launched while the Jap envoys
in Washington, Nomura and Kurusu, were stalling for time. No
accurate estimate of dead or damage available. Radio reports show
the country speedily girding for war. Members of the armed services
being called to duty; civilian defenses mobilized; strikes canceled,
as a new spirit of national unity sweeps the country. Calmly, coldly,
quickly, we must organize to wipe out Japan, and probably protect
ourselves from Axis attacks elsewhere. It is here at last, the grim
spectre of a complete World War in which we are to play a vital and
decisive role. Tomorrow Congress will declare war. God sustain our
President, our Congress, the fighting forces and the Nation. We have
got to win—and win we shall! AMEN.

PREFACE

Don Ball, Jr.

AN APPROACH WHISTLE drifts in from out west of town. The thundering exhausts of a fast-moving train are quite audible, although a couple of miles away. In an instant, comparative quiet as throttles are closed on the engines. The roll of a heavy train can still be heard. The agent comes out of the depot onto the platform with an order hoop in each hand—a familiar sight by now. I have been hearing the trains, day in and day out, and it is hard not to go to the depot anytime the opportunity presents itself. Today is no exception. Two Rock Island M-50 class Mountain types round the bend, burnished rods rising and falling in arcs, catching the low morning light, white flags flying on the lead—another extra, bringing more of the boys back home. The two heavy Mountain types grunt to a stop and I am standing next to 210 feet of locomotive—symbolic to me of the power that has defeated the Axis. After the lead locomotive takes water, a noisy drama ensues: wildly slipping drivers, stack talk, a rain of cinders. The ground trembles as the lead and road engines work with each other, jockeying the weight of the train, spotting the road engine's tender next to the water plug. Amid a hubbub of activity, both engineers climb down to the ground to oil around, while trainmen, the head brakeman, and conductor exchange words with the MP's and an escort (a railroad representative who accompanies troop trains) out on the platform in the cool morning air. I learn that this long, jammed-to-capacity train is running as the second section of the *Imperial,* and that railroad people refer to troop trains as "main trains." This train is main 2-39. The conductor comes up to talk to the head end; watches are compared. The waterspout is returned to its standing position and both firemen go to work on their fires. The injector on the lead engine spurts, while pops noisily lift on the road engine. Both engineers get back up into their cabs, and no time is wasted giving the highball. Throttles are opened, cylinder cocks roar, and the tremendous fury of unleashed steam barks through the stacks, the smoke darkening the sky. Sixteen drivers bite hard on the sanded rail, and main 2-39 is on the move, once again a statistic: one of several hundred troop trains on the nation's rails today.

I was too young at the time to be impressed with statistics, but I was certainly awed by the number of trains that were running through town right after the war. "Like trolley cars," the agent said. Close to a million-and-a-half soldiers, sailors, and marines were riding our nation's rails each month! Back to the personnel centers and separation centers; back to staging areas for farther destinations. More GI's were moving over the rails than at any time during the war.

But the railroads were ready. This was the climax of their astonishing wartime effort.

In 1939, although war clearly threatened from the time of Hitler's invasion of Poland on September 1, the United States was reluctant to face the possibility of American involvement. The country was just recovering from the Depression and was looking forward to a bit of comfort; isolationist sentiment in Congress and throughout the nation was strong. But during 1940, as England fought off invasion, the country seemed to be preparing for the inevitable war—if not physically, certainly psychologically. Every morning newspapers gave Americans vivid accounts of the devastation taking place an ocean away—the invasion of Denmark and Norway, the conquest of the Lowlands and France, the Battle of Britain. Edward R. Murrow brought the war into our living rooms, live from London every night: "This . . . is London." Yet many devout isolationists kept believing that the broad ocean would keep hostilities away from home soil, and when President Roosevelt proposed helping arm our badly overmatched allies, cries of "warmonger" rang out from many a camp. Our Army ranked seventeenth in manpower and strength among the armies of the world, and that broad ocean began to look a little smaller. In his 1941 State of the Union message, the President requested $1.8 million to build up our military forces, and in March the Lend-Lease Act, providing goods and services to our allies, was passed. On December 7, America's course was abruptly determined, and for the next forty-five months the greatest all-out mobilization of men, matériel, and resources the world had ever known took place in the United States.

Even as the Battle of Britain raged—over a year before the United States entered the war—enormous, powerful locomotives were rolling off the erection-shop floors of Baldwin, Lima, American Locomotive, and Electro Motive, and so were mighty "home-builds" on many railroads. Gargantuan 1,131,675-pound articulateds for the Duluth, Mesabi & Iron Range, designed to haul iron ore for our steel mills single-handedly, were on the boards at Baldwin, while at Lima, the most powerful four-cylinder, six-coupled articulateds ever built were being readied for the Chesapeake & Ohio. American Locomotive was completing the first units of an order for the Union Pacific—of locomotives so huge that a worker at the plant chalked the name "Big Boy," along with a *V* for victory, on the smokebox of the first one. The name stuck. At Electro Motive, the first true locomotive assembly line was mass producing 5,400-horse-power diesel freighters, designated only by the letter classification "FT"—and by the paint schemes of the various railroads. A visitor walking into any one of these great locomotive plants would have found encouraging insight into America's production capacity.

The railroads were already entering high-gear war production. At Baldwin, along with those blueprints for the DM&IR articulateds, were plans for the biggest gun mounts ever built, for machined tools for aircraft factories, for ship propellers and a 500-ton keel bender for Victory Ships. At Lima, where precision machining was an art, requests were coming from Uncle Sam for parts—from A to Z. At Alco, the top-secret M-7 mobile 105-mm gun was being produced—the weapon that eventually drove Rommel into retreat across North Africa to Cape Bon. Along with the locomotives and the M-7, Alco was building M-3 medium tanks, the M-4 Sherman, marine boilers, and just about anything else asked of the company, be it a killer tank, or parts for Corsairs, Hellcats, or Avengers. At Electro Motive, the first all-welded tank hulls were sharing floor space with the FT's, along with engines for LCI's (Landing Craft, Infantry), LST's (Landing Ship, Tank), and Army tugs.

America was becoming the "arsenal of democracy." In March 1941, sixteen tanks were constructed under the Lend-Lease Act; by September, over 28,000 American-built tanks had been sent to Britain! Our industries produced equally staggering amounts of supplies for all our allies—$51 billion worth. *All* of these supplies moved from the home front to the battlefield wholly or in part over the rails of our nation. For the railroads, their mightiest hour had begun.

I can't remember clearly—I was too young—the incredible transformation that took place *overnight* on our railroads, turning those twin ribbons of steel into an iron warpath. And so I leave that story to Rogers Whitaker, who was an officer in the Traffic Control Center of the Transportation Corps in the Pentagon, which had the task of coordinating troop trains, military freight, and casuals (small groups). My own memories are of radio reports, blackouts, air raid precautions, food stamps—and trains! My most vivid memories are nocturnal. All night long, miles and miles away across the sleeping land, trains could be heard, one after another. Redball freights, rocketing passenger trains, and troop extras—whistling, thundering, keeping the rails hot. And by day, those haughty, black, burly engines banged on through town, bringing the GI-in-olive almost too close for comfort. The main trains, by and large, were solid Pullman consists, sometimes running as sections of regular trains, or as extras, flying white. The trains came by in consists of makeshift troop sleepers, hospital cars, tourist sleepers, coaches—you name it. And I remember the incredibly long freights, thundering on each other's markers. Those who heard the trains realized the unbelievable momentum of the nation's war machine. Those who stood by the tracks felt that everything we could build and throw at the Axis was rushing past. As each train approached there was the sense that the war depended on *that* train! And any railroader would tell you that those locomotives were hot as pistols, steaming beautifully. Railroad men and women up and down the line felt enormous pride knowing that the railroads would help destroy the adversary and forge the peace.

The railroads went to war with undaunted spirit. Company advertisements proclaimed eventual Allied victory right from the start—never "if," but "when." The railroads rallied with iron resolve. The Sante Fe proudly called its huge new steamers and diesel freight locomotives "battlewagons"; Boston & Maine reminded the public that they were "one of America's railroads, *all* united for Victory," while Great Northern proclaimed that out of the boxcars they hauled, "bombers are born." The Association of American Railroads rightfully called the railroads the "main line of defense," announcing that the freight cars carrying war supplies to the seaports each day had the capacity to carry the daily food for half our population! *It is my hope that this volume will graphically portray what it took to start a war freight every four seconds, and a special troop movement every six minutes.*

Just a word about chapter 4 and the railroad stations: Those stations were standing before "our decade"; most of them still stand—in some form (though a disheartening number have been torn down). But for the stations, too, the period from 1940 to 1950 was a special one. Without them the railroads could not have met the challenges of the decade, could not have operated 113,891 special troop trains, or handled the millions of troops who traveled on scheduled civilian trains. Why, 62,762,860 people passed through Grand Central Terminal in 1944 alone! And certainly at no time were more people packed into the tiny country depots than during the war years; and at no other time was the little station, where men and boys said their good-byes on their way to a far-off war, a more important centerpiece in each town. Chapter 4 was originally planned as "A Day in Union Station," featuring the work of photographer Jack Delano, who was on an Office of War Information assignment in the Chicago station in January 1943. But only part of the story was taking place in Union; a look at the train departure board tells much more, conjuring up faraway cities and their magnificent stations, and the hundreds of smaller stations and depots along the way. So the chapter evolved. Too little is ever shown of railroad stations; here is an opportunity to see their infinite variety—here is the *very look* of railroading, from its pioneering days of ingenuity and conquest.

I hope this book captures the spirit of railroading in the forties and also the unique character (the term "mood" suggests something too temporary) of America during the war and the rest of the decade. During the 1940s, America "worked." It seemed to be an era of good times and almost innocent merriment—even with the dark and terrible war. Such opposed ideologies as isolationism and interventionism somehow managed to coexist without terrorist bombings, social clashes, or public hearings. The forties were, as some say, *natural*—without pretense or guile. The forties were a time of much fun and foolishness—fun and foolishness that has all but disappeared in today's hectic "where-are-we-going?" world. Still, "responsibility" was a meaningful term in the forties; *no one* forgot Pearl Harbor and the fact that a job had to be done. But when the jukeboxes and radios played the Andrews Sisters' "Don't Sit under the Apple Tree" or Glenn Miller's "String of Pearls," it was time to enjoy (yet not waste) life. And when those same jukeboxes and radios played "Praise the Lord and Pass the Ammunition"—well, a job had to be done. America's pride, friendliness, grace, and meaning were never for a moment lost during the war (ironically, that happened in peacetime).

The forties: Betty Grable's gams, Frank Sinatra's voice, Joe DiMaggio's bat. Jitterbugging; red, red lips; bobby socks. Mel Allen's "Ballantine Blast," "*Life* Goes to a Party," *Esquire*'s pinup girls. The forties—a pleasing ring to it all. But "a slip of the lip may sink a ship." Fun—meaningful work—and a war on our hands.

Something of this spirit comes out in many of the photographs by Jack Delano that appear in this book—a feeling of friendliness, yet firm dedication to the task at hand. (Delano's Union Station picture story was not an isolated assignment; he had been delegated by the Office of War Information to document in photographs the railroads' wartime activities.)

Not every picture in this book was taken during the war, but every one *does* represent the railroad scene during that decade. The book is an attempt to portray the *total* railroad picture during the war and the later forties. In a way, the project stems from a love for the 1940s era; above all, it grows from a longtime desire to tell the great behind-the-scenes story—the human side of railroading. *Decade of the Trains* is a tribute to the railroads of America.

One of my first photos — Union Pacific westbound through Lawrence, Kansas, July 1946. (BALL)

PROLOGUE

Rogers E. M. Whitaker

AN EXTREMELY ENTHUSIASTIC snowstorm along the southern shore of Lake Erie had made the first weekend of December a preview of Christmas, and a few of those to whom the railway is mankind's most magnificent achievement were making the best possible use of an unexpected brief holiday. In their warm hotel in Jamestown, New York, they were planning an excursion along the full length of the Jamestown, Westfield & Northwestern, an interurban line that in its great days had carried swarms of summer vacationers along Lake Chautauqua, had carried the United States mails faster and better than any vehicle the Post Office can muster on that route today, and that was still carrying, in the final years of its useful life, the likes of that small group of enthusiasts. Cameras in hand, they hoped soon to be on their way to the other end of the line, at Westfield, New York, alongside Lake Erie, where they were to photograph the New York Central's brand-new, streamlined version of its *Empire State Express* as it stopped in Westfield on its very first run, from Cleveland through Buffalo to New York City. They would then ride the train all the way

home to New York. But late Saturday night word came to Jamestown that, for unexplained reasons, the new train would begin its eastward run in Buffalo instead of Cleveland. The only way to preview the new *Empire State* would be to catch an earlier, slower train out of Cleveland when it called at Westfield and go on to Buffalo.

It was dark and snowing when the small band assembled at the interurban station to board the first train of the day from Jamestown to Westfield—a single car on that gloomy Sunday, but warm enough for comfort. Halfway along its winding descent of the broad escarpment that sloped north toward Westfield and Lake Erie, the car took to the side track at a tiny station perched beside a crossroads, and suddenly rude noises and a slight sidewise lurch announced that the train had run aground off the icebound rails. The only man aboard in high boots dropped off the train and waddled as rapidly as he could along the highway to find a farmhouse telephone. Forty minutes later a taxi miraculously appeared to ferry the group to Westfield—to arrive one minute before the train to Buffalo pulled in. That was the last time any of the young men in that group would ever see their favorite interurban (it died of malnutrition a few years later), and the events then under way elsewhere—unknown to them at the time—would soon so change their lives that none of them would ever see any of the others again.

But they were a happy group at midday on that weather-bound Sunday when they came alongside the platform at Buffalo Central Terminal, from which the new *Empire State Express* would commence its truncated run to Grand Central Terminal. They were happy even though there was no time to push through the assemblage of admiring welcomers to photograph the handsomely streamlined steam engine—one of New York Central's classic 4-6-4 Hudsons; instead, they all raced to the rear to inspect the observation car. The most conservative of the travelers had with regret informed his companions en route that the new observation car was not, as it had been for so many years, a stately and weighty Pullman parlor car, with an open platform, properly brass-railed and awninged, with stately and commodious swiveling armchairs in which those travelers with enough foresight (and cash) to have reserved accommodations had traditionally made their royal progress across New York State. Although the observation car of the newly hatched *Empire* was glittery and accommodating, it was no longer a patrician Pullman, but instead a vehicle open to all. Almost as alarming, the new parlor cars were up at the head end, where in better times only the baggagemaster would have been exiled. "The winds of change," muttered the senior traveler from Jamestown as he boarded the observation day coach.

The sparse turnout at the Buffalo station—and, indeed, on the train itself—was not what one would have expected on such a notable occasion as the birthday of the new *Empire State Express;* and the comparatively modest collection of greeters at Buffalo was succeeded by a still smaller one at Rochester. So it went along the line all the way to Albany, where the explanation finally caught up with the travelers: Pearl Harbor had been bombed that day, December 7, 1941.

The winds of change—or, really, the winds of adversity—that already had been blowing for a quarter of a century across the right-of-way of the railroads of this country had not yet attained gale force

(that was not to happen until the 1970s), but their strength had been gathering since the end of the First World War. Thirty-six years after that momentous Sunday in 1941, a documentarian can draw upon only isolated memories. The history of the uneasy relationship between war and railroading is brief—but it is basic. War historically has a paradoxical effect upon railroading: it stimulates that industry to perform far beyond the level industry leaders think possible, and at the same time it destroys the railroads, in a variety of ways.

The consensus of military commentators is that our own Civil War was the first conflict in which the railways were of importance. And during that war, for every man who was getting unprecedented performance from the locomotive he drove or the right-of-way he tended, there was a counterpart ripping up ties and turning them into bonfires, or heating rails in the flames until they could be wound like tape around telegraph poles so that they would be forevermore useless. The railroads' effect on combat did not go unnoticed. Even the French—whom military strategists consider to be virtually the inventors of the "art" of war (army terminology bristles with words originating in the military history of France)—sent observers to follow the course of our Civil War; and the Germans and the British, equally eager to study fresh techniques, had their observers on the battlefields, too. The United States government itself pondered the Civil War's lessons on the uses of the railway in wartime. During the war, for instance, an uprising of Confederate irregulars in the Far West had posed a difficult problem because that region was then accessible only by horseback across the plains and mountains beyond the Mississippi, or by ship around Cape Horn. One of the first plans carried to fruition after the war was the building of railway lines to complete the transcontinental network. One line moved west from Omaha, one moved east from Sacramento, until they met in 1869 at Promontory Point, Utah. The ravaged rights-of-way, the blown-up railway bridges, the intentionally derailed locomotives and cars that were the relics of the Civil War were soon replaced, and fifty years of exuberant—and not always wholly necessary—railway construction began, halted but temporarily now and then by this or that economic crisis. Each crisis was, of course, induced in part by that unnecessary railway construction. But year by year over that long span, the railway network grew. The Spanish-American War, a brief and largely naval conflict, had no considerable effect on the railways, and at the time the country entered the First World War, the American railways were almost all in robust health. The word *abandonment* had not yet made its sinister way into the railway lexicon.

The First World War did add a word, however: *priority*. The huge Hog Island shipyards that were set up near Philadelphia to build the fleet of ugly-duckling but absolutely essential wartime freighters were receiving their materials pell-mell. The manufacturers of anchors and hawsers were turning out their specialities with such diligence, and the railways were hauling them to Hog Island with such speed that the shipyards were choked with cars loaded with anchors and hawsers when what was needed was steel to lay keels and plates to construct the hulls of the vessels. An arm of the federal government, designated the United States Railroad Administration (USRA), had to step in to set up priorities. The agency had to resolve many situations of that sort; it even had to arrange for assembling a flotilla of streetcars sizable enough to transport the thousands of men who were working at Hog Island. The USRA, which was dissolved after the war, experienced huge and complex problems and they were not always solved effectively; now and again, even today, that agency's performance is cited as proof that the federal government should not interfere with the conduct of private business. This argument conveniently overlooks the fact that many of the men in the upper reaches of the USRA were railway officials who simply changed titles—and sometimes changed from mufti into uniform—but went on sitting at desks they had always sat at and went on doing just about the same jobs.

The battlefields of 1914–1918 were thousands of miles away overseas, and there was no heating and twisting of rails in this country, no dynamiting of bridges; the tiny amount of sabotage that was accomplished was the handiwork of a scattering of singularly inept German sympathizers. Mostly what had to be repaired was the damage done to rails, to cars, to locomotives, and to signaling devices that had been worked overtime during the war; and even after the war, other priorities—relating to the use of many kinds of material—had to be extended for a time until mills and factories that had been turned

over to the war industries could be brought back into the civilian economy.

But there was even greater, less tangible, damage to the railroads. A state of war stimulates not only railroading but other sectors of industry as well to extraordinary efforts. The internal-combustion engine was put to a multiplicity of new tasks during the First World War—in heavy-duty army trucks, in armored tanks, in aircraft—and the refinements built into successive variants of this engine had significant results: more horsepower was developed per pound, less fuel burned per horsepower produced. These improvements in the internal-combustion engine would ultimately have serious consequences for railroading.

The roads, too, were affected. Even at the time of the First World War, many of the highways were still dirt roads, and they followed every contour of the land; the minor reconstruction occasionally necessitated by the lightly burdened vehicles that traveled them was often performed by the farmers who lived along the roads: in lieu of paying county taxes, the farmers "worked off" their taxes (the phrase is theirs) by donating themselves, a team of horses, a wagon, and occasionally an able-bodied son, for however many days the county clerk thought proper. That all began to change after the war. The Scot who gave his name to the pavement called macadam made a major contribution to the development of the first truly year-round competitor of the railways. The steadily improving versions of the internal-combustion engine were now being installed in buses that traveled the steadily improving roads. It was too early in our history to describe the rivalry that ensued between road and rail as a "cold war," but cold war it was.

And the end was inevitable. The history of the ways man has found to move across the face of the earth shows the inevitable triumph of the new, the convenient, and the swift over the old modes. The plodder on foot gave way to the man on horseback, who gave way to the driver of the stagecoach, who gave way to the pilot of the river steamboat and the skipper of the canal packet boat. These gave way to the locomotive engineer, and for a very long time it seemed impossible that any other invention could affect the health or wealth of his imposing machine. But the locomotive engineer, too, eventually had to give way.

It is not the purpose of this narrative to enumerate all the ills—political, legislative, economic—that from this time on assailed the railway industry from without, nor to list the varied and ingenious knaveries that assailed it from within. Its purpose at this point is to set forth the reasons for the widespread doubt that the railway industry of the United States was in a fit state to take on the huge extra weight imposed upon it that snowy December day in 1941.

What had appeared to be a perennial expansion of the railway trackage in the United States had come to an end almost simultaneously with the end of the First World War. Here and there, naturally, logging lines and mining lines had closed down over the years, but now the growth halted everywhere: the unpleasant word *abandonment* had come into frequent use. The closing of the Colorado Midland, the first large-scale cessation of activity in United States railway history, took place in 1916. Thenceforth, the route mileage of the American railway system grew smaller year by year. A shortage of railway coal and a shortage of railway locomotives during the First World War had persuaded the USRA that a number of passenger trains should be combined; this was one fiat that appealed to certain railway managements, for freight trains were a better source of income, and the industry was thus inclined to continue this arrangement after the war had ended. When an official of the New York Central (then one of the country's largest haulers of passengers) was asked whether he planned to restore its passenger services in New England to their speedy and convenient prewar state, he answered, "Forty miles an hour is fast enough for anyone."

In any case, the railroads had ways of taking care of punier competitors. The New York, New Haven & Hartford, for example, simply bought any conflicting interurban line that would take its money, as well as all passenger steamship lines that plied the New England coast toward Boston. The large railroads' territorial imperative seemed supreme. The Boston & Albany, mildly challenged by a wispy interurban that ran parallel to it from West Warren to Spencer through Brookfield (all of them comfortably well-to-do Massachusetts country towns), waited while the interurban put up its new generating plant alongside the railway a few miles east of Brookfield and then informed the management of the interurban that the

B&A would not install a siding at the generating plant—the coal required would have to be unloaded at Brookfield and carted, all expenses paid by the interurban, to the generating plant. So much for competition from the interurbans!

But its was not the interurbans that were the threat. The men who were putting better internal-combustion engines into buses and automobiles, and now trucks, did not agree that forty miles an hour was fast enough. The cold war grew colder. The bus and the automobile nibbled at the passenger train; soon the truck was nibbling at the freight train. Once, milk had come down to New York City from northern Vermont or even from across the Saint Lawrence, in Canada, in trains that belied the poky image of the "milk train": the train that hauled milk from the utmost reaches of Vermont to the Borden Company plant on the west side of New York City was the fastest run on the Rutland Railroad, of fond memory, upon which it commenced its journey. Milk is a high-income earner for whoever moves it, and the truck began to pick off this valuable traffic. Other perishables followed—vegetables, fruit, cattle. Soon after the nation's greatest economic crisis began in 1929, perhaps a third of the railway trackage in the country was in the bankruptcy courts. The federal Reconstruction Finance Corporation had to resurrect the lines with bountiful loans.

If a documentarian wished to recreate on film that innocent journey from Jamestown to New York City on December 7, 1941, shooting on location could not be managed. Jamestown still sits high on the north bank of a river valley, beside the passenger station on the main line of the late Erie Railroad (later called the Erie-Lackawanna). From that station came many passengers who continued their journey across town at the station of the Jamestown, Westfield & Northwestern. They did, that is, until the town council, asserting that the interurban cars that trundled along the street to a corner near the Erie station were obstructing traffic, ordered the interurban to move to the western end of town—a goodly hike for anyone not burdened by luggage, and a practically compulsory taxicab ride for anyone who was. Thus the course of "integrated" transport in this country! The automobiles that parked along both sides of the street down which the interurbans traveled did not, it appears, obstruct traffic. The interurban is gone. The documentarian would find only its path—where it wandered to Lake Chautauqua and slid down the little hill into Westfield before it turned sharply east to reach the New York Central station. But today there is only one passenger train passing each way through Westfield, and it no longer stops there.

And the most important performer in the documentary? The new *Empire State Express* unveiled in 1941 exceeded in handsomeness anything the New York Central had ever invented. If something had to replace the old *Empire State Express,* this train was it. Even the steady customers—the politicians, the legislators, the lobbyists who traveled in it to and from the capital at Albany—had to concede that the new parlor cars, even though they were placed ignominiously up at the head end, were more than acceptable. The slightly solemn interiors of the old Pullmans—Pullman decorators were extraordinarily fond of dark greens—had given way to interiors in sunnier hues; the wall-to-wall carpeting was similarly cheerful; in place of the earlier seats that swiveled about with such ease that many a small boy had turned his into a merry-go-round when his parents weren't looking were armchairs of a vastness and comfort that would have made them quite at home beside a picture window in the Union League Club.

A trifle astern of the parlor car and its delights was the dining car, in which, though times were no longer so grand as they had been, the masterpiece of the breakfast table was still sole—not fillet of sole from the deep freeze, but whole sole from the Fulton Fish Market. According to a dining-car steward of the 1940s, on the opening day of legislative sessions in Albany more than forty soles met a glorious doom in the dining car on the way from Grand Central Terminal to Albany. The day coaches that lay ahead of the dining-car pleasure dome offered their guests a generous portion of leg room, a generous portion of properly stuffed upholstery; the observation car afforded not merely such commonplaces as packets of salted peanuts but, during the hours when they were legal, fortified liquids.

But what remains of that glory? Nearly all of the objects that made up that wonderful caravan, two or three city blocks long, have vanished. The Hudson that drew the train out of Buffalo that day in December 1941 was long ago cut up for scrap. Not one of her sister locomotives—exemplars of a high-speed machine that became famous for its stalwart performance and that was copied the world around—survives. Searchers of files believe that one or two of the coaches are alive and fairly well in Mexico; no one can find the observation car. One of the parlor cars, the Herbert H. Lehman, reappeared briefly a few years ago in the consist of a morning commuter train from Philadelphia to New York—the last certified remnant of the *Empire State Express. Sic transit gloria!*

In December 1941 the *Empire State Express* and her sister streamlined trains that were rolling across other parts of the United States were proclaimed heralds of the Dawn of a New Era for the railways. The railways and the trains that rode upon them were here to stay. Yet, as this country moved steadily toward a state of war there were men in the back rooms of railway offices, and not a few in the board rooms, who were pondering the question of whether their organizations could support the extra burden that would be laid upon them by war. In the shadows behind the glittery new passenger trains were the ghosts of many other passenger trains—and not all of them minor—that had been disappearing one by one over the years. Rather than "Dawn of a New Era," a more appropriate cliché for the *Empire State Express* itself might have been "shadow of its former self."

Even in its latter days the original *Empire State Express* had been a grand old lady (a grand old *heavyweight* lady, with all those ninety- and ninety-five-ton vehicles), and it had proudly denied its parochial name—the *Empire State* was an international train four times over. Beginning the journey with it out of Grand Central Terminal were a parlor car and one or two coaches amidships that were to be detached at Albany, there to form part of the *Green Mountain Flyer,* which then commenced its day-long passage over the rails of the New York Central, the Troy Union, the Boston & Maine, the Rutland, and the Canadian National into Montreal. At Utica a parlor car, and sometimes a coach, would be set out by the *Empire State* for the Adirondack service of the New York Central, which later split two ways: one bit of it, with the parlor car, headed for Lake Placid; another bit of it, to which another parlor car had been added at Utica, traveled to the Canadian border and on into Montreal—the last few miles of its sprint over rails of the Canadian Pacific into Windsor Station. Thus, the *Empire State* magnificently served two passenger stations in Montreal.

At Buffalo the train underwent major surgery: coaches and a brace of parlor cars for Cleveland; a similar assortment for the rails of the Michigan Central across lower Ontario; and a coach and the open-platform observation/parlor car going north into Ontario on the rails of the New York Central, the Grand Trunk Western (only a few feet of this), the International Bridge & Railway Company, the Toronto, Hamilton & Buffalo, the Hamilton Terminal Railways, the Canadian Pacific (a barely noticeable sliver of this), the Canadian National, and the Toronto Terminal Railways.

The end of the run of the observation car was sometimes incongruous: at Hamilton, the Canadian Pacific's Hamilton-Montreal sleeping car was occasionally attached at the rear end, thus blocking the view of the hardy voyagers who stuck it out through cinders and soot for the final forty-odd miles of the run into Toronto. As compensation, though, a foresighted railway buff who had booked himself a bedroom in that sleeping car could begin his journey in the observation car and then walk across the open platform and into the sleeper after the train had departed from Hamilton, thereby traveling from New York to Montreal on a route totaling more than 870 miles (the shortest route is under 400 miles) without ever stepping off his train. All this on a round-trip fare—and there were indeed buffs who spent a sumptuous weekend in this fashion; it was such almost-nonstop passengers who helped keep the American railways well funded in their best days. But these dedicated passengers would have to accept their new lot—the demise of such a grand-circle route between New York and Montreal, the demise of the open-platform observation/parlor car, the demise of their pleasure-bent railroad weekends—and they did so with sorrow for a splendid past and with determination to apply themselves to new ways of living. They, the United States, and the railways were at war.

Above, wartime *Empire State Express* blasts through Oscawana, New York.
Opposite: Highball!—westward from Harmon. (NOWAK)

1

THE

IRON

TRAIL

THE TRAIL LED EVERYWHERE, or nearly everywhere, in spite of the helter-skelter pattern of abandonments that had for a quarter of a century been eating away at the fabric of the American railway network. Now, even though the United States was at war, it was often business as usual. The daily, the three-times-a-week, the once-a-week mixed train continued to ply its trade wherever it was useful for the war effort; just as often, though, the old familiar routine disappeared. Railways that had been moribund for years were reincarnated. The Kansas City, Kaw Valley & Western, whose straggling catenary suggested that it had long ago expired, enjoyed a certain renewal of life when the federal government set up, at Bonner Springs, Kansas, a huge munitions plant—huge enough to relieve temporarily the frowns of the railway's two trustees in bankruptcy. The Rapid City, Black Hills & Western—whose daily-except-Sunday passenger train managed to stagger over its thirty-four miles of track west from Rapid City, South Dakota, to an interchange with the Burlington in the minute town of Mystic in less than 2½ hours—experienced a vast increase in

customers; the Army Air Force, which had established a base in the high terrain above Rapid City, had discovered that the line was a handy way of moving its personnel to and from that base.

Some of the decisions about accommodating the shifting of personnel—civilian as well as military—for the innumerable burgeoning government installations were made on site, but as the realization grew that the war would not be an overnight affair, it became apparent that a master control must be arranged so that the on-site decisions would not conflict with one another. So it was that the Office of Defense Transportation (ODT), the equivalent of the United States Railroad Administration of the First World War, evolved to supervise the movement of civilian traffic. So it was that the hastily set-up Traffic Control (TC) sector of the venerable Army Transportation Corps (which, quaintly, found itself berthed inside the Quartermaster Corps) burgeoned out of practically nothing—a few ramshackle offices in an old government building just north of Pennsylvania Avenue in Washington—into an organization whose headquarters alone spread over a fair share of the Pentagon and whose outposts covered the country from coast to coast, from north to south, and even appeared in western Canada (for the overland route to Alaska, a possible target for Japanese invasion, was through Canada).

The need for a form of "traffic control" was far more pressing than it had been during the First World War, and not merely because this was the biggest war yet. The inventive mind is ever spurred by the presence of menace; machines and devices, both aggressive and defensive, were being planned and put into production at a rate that was to astound not only the United States but the rest of the world as well—not least, the Axis. As civilian factories appeared to turn out the war machinery, dependent communities sprang into existence like mushrooms after a heavy rainfall, and many of them included military establishments—training posts, warehouses, and the like—that had sprouted just as suddenly. The task of assuring that the thousands of daily movements between all these points would not weave themselves into a gigantic snarl fell to the Transportation Corps' Traffic Control. The brass of Traffic Control and the overseers of its civilian counterpart, the ODT, held weekly meetings over lunch in a downtown Washington hotel to work out coordinates. And none too soon. The Official Guides of 1942 list more than three hundred military installations in the United States. They do not list the myriad installations known only to those who *needed* to know. The Air Force was especially secretive regarding the whereabouts of some of its installations. Accordingly, the railroad men who had been hauled out of civilian life and put to work in Traffic Control headquarters became accustomed to long-distance calls from mystified vice-presidents of big manufacturing firms. A typical conversation might begin: "I've got three hot cars of aircraft motors on my siding for an Air Force layout in Texas, and they won't tell me where the layout is. How am I supposed to route the cars?" Well, no war machine is perfect, but ours did its best: a Traffic Control railroad man would get an Air Force colonel on the intercom and lay bare one or two facts of life; the aircraft motors would be routed, and would arrive on time.

Matters could have been much worse. But the Office of Defense Transportation was headed by Joseph Eastman, the most intelligent and innovative transportation man ever to hold a government post

in this country—and his main assistants were John W. Barriger, the most intelligent and innovative railway official in the country, and H. A. McCarthy, the brains of the passenger-traffic department of the Boston & Maine. (This railway was the precursor of the intermodal systems that are much talked about but rarely set up today: the Boston & Maine ran passenger trains, passenger buses, and a passenger airline.) And Traffic Control imported—not without certain demurs from within—a small, seemingly mild, definitely unassuming, and incredibly patient civilian, Arthur H. Gass, from the Association of American Railroads. And from the inland waterways Traffic Control inherited a gruff but efficient civilian, Kenneth Rutger, who had run one of the biggest barge lines on the Mississippi. There were intercity truckmen, too, within the Traffic Control compound; for once, the angry rivalry between train, truck, and barge was relaxed.

Military protocol suggested that such important civilians within Traffic Control should become part of the military—"so you can deal with colonels and generals on an equal footing"—but Gass and Rutger held out for civilian status, and before long a cordial and even admiring relationship between civilian and military came to pass. There were career military men, too, in the Transportation Corps. In Traffic Control, young officers such as Colonel E. C. R. Lasher and Colonel I. Sewell Morris, West Point graduates who deserved the appellation "gentleman and scholar," had had to learn their logistics trade by proxy—as observers, for instance, of the railway operations that hauled and fed thousands of Boy Scouts for their annual Jamboree, moving them thousands of miles across the country to their encampment. There was far more to be learned as the Transportation Corps and its Traffic Control expanded. Army man and civilian sat down together to learn—the Army man to say what he needed done, the civilian to tell him how it could be accomplished. Official notes were taken at all these conclaves—notes that were to be expanded into a manual for future learners. The note-takers held that the manual should be called "How to Win a World War." They were right.

Cooperation, cooperation, always cooperation. A typical problem: A branch of the military set up an educational facility at Hamilton College, in the small upstate-New York town of Clinton. Oil tankers were slipping into the Atlantic with holes torn in their flanks by German torpedoes at an alarming rate at the time, and the rationing of gasoline had begun. The problem was how to move graduates and new arrivals at the changing of the shifts between Clinton and Utica, ten or so miles away, without using scarce gasoline. The New York, Ontario & Western, whose picturesque but leisurely passenger trains had already deserted that part of the world, still rolled freight through Clinton, so the track was still there. First a word from Traffic Control to the Office of Defense Transportation, then another word to the trustee in bankruptcy of the Ontario & Western—and soon a passenger service between Clinton and Utica commenced, on the days the military wanted. The little trains snuffled their way to and from the forecourt of the old Lackawanna station in Utica, which was but a short walk to the New York Central station and connecting lines.

Similarly: Fort Dix, a dozen miles outside of Trenton, New Jersey, was a clearinghouse for enormous numbers of soldiers. Many of them arrived at the base in long troop trains, or "main moves," as the military called them. But so many passenger trains—from the Northeast, from the Deep South, from the Midwest—called at Trenton every day that "casuals" (what the military called groups of fewer than twenty or thirty GI's) were constantly alighting in the city, with no means to reach the army base. Could not the Pennsylvania Railroad, in order to save gasoline, run a train every midafternoon from Trenton to Fort Dix for these casuals? It could, and it did. For the assistance of transport officers in military installations all over the country, that train was listed in the public timetable. The station in Trenton was within civilian territory, but the "station" in Fort Dix was in military territory, where "unauthorized personnel" were not welcome, so the ticket agents in Trenton were told not to sell tickets to adventurous railway buffs or to any other civilians. An inspection of the train by the military police shortly before departure ensured that no civilians had slipped through the lines. The most observant buffs, noting that the timetables offered no return train to Trenton, were able to guess that the train was indeed not a public one.

Steps were taken to meet the menacing problems created by the torpedoing of the oil tankers. There were already trains serving as long-haul pipelines

for oil traffic, and another line—from Texas to the Northeast—was rapidly put in operation. But now the long lines of railway tank cars that had sat desolate and forgotten on rusting side tracks for years had to be put back into service again. The coast-to-coast traffic from the wineries of California to the "châteaux" in the Bronx, where the wine was bottled for the retail trade, ceased; the porcelain-lined tank cars in which these goods had traveled were assigned to hauling liquids of a far greater potency and infinitely less palatability.

Other problems, too, were adjusted by conference within Traffic Control's walls or at the weekly meetings in downtown Washington. Freight transportation was needed to a plant converted to military production that lay along the segment of the New York, Ontario & Western between West Cornwall and Middletown, in New York State. The O&W, as traffic declined, had set aside a number of its museum-piece cars, but all of these had already been preempted by another military operation: a commuter train to haul the personnel of the colossal Martin bomber plant—located alongside the main line of the Pennsylvania Railroad—to and from Baltimore at shift-change time. So O&W stock was unavailable, but the Rutland Railroad, which had spent most of its life falling upon hard times, had recently fallen on another of them, and some of its local trains were now extinct. So a new train soon appeared between West Cornwall and Middletown made up of Rutland coaches, still bearing their true owner's legend, and another situation was saved.

One job of the Office of Defense Transportation was to be on constant lookout for rail that was underused. The abandonment of railway lines that would become so frequent in the 1970s was taking place during the Second World War, too, but on a more modest scale. The eyes of the ODT in time fell upon a stretch of Seaboard Air Line trackage that sloped away southwest from Tallahassee, the capital of Florida, toward a dot on the map beside the Gulf of Mexico named Carrabelle. The Seaboard Air Line had long ago ceased to wonder why on earth it had ever built such an unproductive branch, and was now quite content to let the ODT reclaim the rail so that it could be used elsewhere. But on this occasion the ODT didn't get the rail. Cooperation—and military priority—came into play again: the Transportation Corps, notified that the ODT needed the Carrabelle rail, replied that Carrabelle would soon be the site of a military training installation the Army did not wish to discuss in public; the track stayed.

Another time it was the Navy that thwarted the plans of acquisitive ODT men. Southward across the Great American Desert ran track maintained for an occasional small freight train, which hauled a wooden day coach on its rear carrying a still more occasional passenger. At midday, when the desert heat was nearing its venomous zenith, the train would halt beside a tiny (and miraculous, in that scene) pond that supported a few trees and a few resolute ducks. It occurred to a few ODT officials that the leisurely and infrequent train and the rails on which it traveled were of vast unimportance. But the Navy intervened to halt the ODT takeover: not far from where the train crew lunched once or twice a week, on a spur track that looked as casual as could be, a repository for naval ammunition lay beneath the desert sands—only an overnight trip away from the West Coast if something there went wrong. The branch line stayed intact until the Japanese had capitulated.

Another segment of trackage the ODT had eyes on was part of the Missouri Pacific Railway's empire in Louisiana. The rail lay between Shreveport and Alexandria, alongside its main line between Shreveport and New Orleans—specifically, it was a long but secondary loop line that began at Reisor, a tiny junction not far south of Shreveport, and rejoined the main line, which ran eastward of it, at the town of Cypress. The towns along this secondary line still rejoiced in, but by no means supported, a local passenger train, and the volume of freight traffic that passed along the line was negligible. The Missouri Pacific's main line, on the other hand, was more than busy—the Deep South's climate meant that troops could be in training maneuvers all day long even in the middle of what the Southland thought, in its innocence, was the dead of winter. Moreover, New Orleans was a port of embarkation of major significance. The rails from the secondary line were expendable and would come in handy, so the ODT began to move in on it. But Traffic Control wanted the line to stay put.

Traffic Control had a special reason, concerned not only with the movement of troops and freight but with the cost of moving them. Back in the nineteenth century, when the federal government

had wanted to expedite the building of privately owned railways it needed for strategic or economic purposes, it had made large grants of land along the desired routes, specifying that in return the railroads must agree to haul the military and its matériel over these lines without charge. This arrangement continued until after the First World War, when the government decided that these land-grant railroads could charge the military half the going rate. The Missouri Pacific loop line between Reisor and Cypress was a land-grant railway and thus became involved in an ingenious scheme to save the military money—a scheme that was being planned by some of the railway men in Traffic Control, most of them rate clerks who had been recruited from civilian life.

Their proposition was this: Over the thousand miles between the vast industrial center Chicago and the vast port of embarkation New Orleans stretched a variety of railway routes—railways in competition not only among themselves, but also vying with the steamships and the barge lines that plied the canals and the Mississippi. None of these were land-grant railways, but in the course of the years some had acquired bits and pieces of railways that had begun as land-grant lines. So on a huge map at Traffic Control the rate clerks worked out a wholly new and completely imaginary railway line between Chicago and New Orleans. It veered back and forth from the trackage of one railway company to that of another, taking in all the land-grant tangents of track along the way. If dim memory is correct, the planners came up with a railway line 35.7 percent of whose mileage was land-grant trackage. They then argued that since land-grant mileage entitled the military to a 50 percent cut in rates, the route plotted entitled them to a reduction of half that 35.7 percent—or a 17.85 percent discount on every man in uniform, every ton of military commodities, hauled between Chicago and New Orleans. Moreover, all railways that paralleled this mythical line, even if they were not the beneficiaries of any land grants, would feel pressured to allow the same 17.85 percent discount to the military. One of the land-grant snippets the rate clerks included in their plot was that secondary loop line of the Missouri Pacific between Reisor and Cypress that the ODT coveted, and because they were afraid its disappearance would jeopardize their scheme, they resisted the ODT's plans. (The railways' reaction to the 35.7 scheme is unprintable—but Traffic Control did ultimately effect a downward adjustment of military rates on all routes between Chicago and New Orleans.)

Military traffic on the railways created other problems. Secrecy is automatic in the military mind in wartime, and officials decided that what supplies were being loaded into the freight cars allotted to certain factories was nobody else's business. But in order for the rate clerks to establish under what "commodity rate" matériel belonging to the military was to be moved, it was necessary for the clerks to know what was in those freight cars. And it was doubly necessary for someone in Traffic Control to know whether the contents of freight cars were likely to explode if they became very warm or if they were given a severe jolt in transit. Such cargo might have to be handled in special trains and over routes that would bypass the centers of big cities. Once more, military and civilian personnel sat down together and made the requisite adjustment.

Other adjustments of this sort frequently had to be worked out. Either to find sufficient space or for reasons of safety, many of the proliferating war plants and military facilities had to be set up well beyond the outskirts of the big towns (which were, after all, the main sources of the supply of men and women who would staff the operations). Traffic Control and the ODT would perform a coordinated task in such a situation: TC would cajole the railways into enlarging the "switch limits" around cities to embrace these war-related operations, thus letting them escape the extra charges railways often imposed for moving freight cars beyond those limits; ODT would arrange public transportation for the employees of these inconveniently located operations.

The Kansas City Public Service Company, which most people thought was merely a quite extensive conglomeration of streetcar lines connecting Kansas City, Missouri, and Kansas City, Kansas, was also a considerable part of the Iron Trail. Its interchange tracks, which led to four or five of the major railways that served the double metropolis, enabled this trolley line to deliver freight to numerous industries in the environs. To the south of the cities a military-supply factory was set up, and the ODT, which had been endowed by law with extraordinary powers of requisition and allocation, immediately had trolley cars trundling out of town along freight tracks to this factory.

A dozen miles north of Minneapolis, the Northern Pump Company had built an enormous plant to supply the military, but there were transportation problems. The tracks of an already shut-down interurban railway, not quite twenty miles in length, still passed by the Northern Pump premises, and that interurban was able to provide the factory with the freight service it needed by making use of diesel locomotives. But transportation for employees was a thornier problem: the cars and engines that made up the old passenger trains had disappeared and had been succeeded by an occasional bus—much too occasional for Northern Pump's personnel requirements. Special service was needed. The Minneapolis trolley-car system, though it was an extensive enterprise, did not extend as far as the tracks of the defunct interurban, so a city bus that passed the downtown Great Northern Railway station along Hennepin Avenue went out toward the northeastern suburbs and came abreast of the tracks that led to Northern Pump. From that point a nondescript passenger train, assembled from the bottom of who knows what barrel by the ODT, carried whatever passengers there were on to the factory. No public mention was made of this service for the workers at Northern Pump—unquestionably because it was intended for them and for no one else, and undoubtedly because no fare was exacted.

The ODT even extended the Iron Trail along city streets. The requisitioning and allocating of buses as well as of trolley cars and trains was within its powers, and buses were commonly provided to serve installations of military interest when no better means of transport were at hand. As for urban trolley lines, the process of shutting them down had attained considerable momentum by the 1940s, but the ODT brought a complete halt to that "March Toward Progress." When Fiorello La Guardia, still mayor of New York City and not yet an officer in the army, sent the ODT a request for a batch of buses to help out urban transit, his order was filled as promptly as possible, but when the ODT discovered that the mayor was using his newly acquired vehicles to replace the venerable but workable trolley cars on the Fifty-ninth Street crosstown line, he was told to put the cars back in service at once and use the buses elsewhere. The trolley cars went back to work for a few more years.

But these urban-transit incursions were just

sidelights to the main job of TC and ODT: moving and monitoring essential freight, essential military, essential civilians throughout the nation. Into a large room in Traffic Control headquarters in the Pentagon reports flowed, once a day or even oftener, on the whereabouts of every troop train, every trainload of matériel. Traffic Control also received intelligence on operations that might affect transport decisions—especially those concerning H&R. *H&R* was Army slang for the complexes of warehouses and sidings that were set up across the country, usually where at least two railways were close at hand so that an interruption of any sort on one line would not put the complex out of action. "Holding and Reconsignment" is the translation, and it meant just that. If a port's docking facilities were crammed with freight cars awaiting the arrival of a fleet of ships, military cargo en route to that port could be put at an H&R installation. The cargo was then on a "holding" status; if a change of route seemed expeditious, "reconsignment" sent the cargo to another port.

The need to acquire a stockpile of locomotives and cars for a win-the-war scheme of such magnitude led the ODT to reorganize certain rituals of civilian life. Moving horses to and from racetracks by rail, and moving the punters who came to bet on them, was discouraged. The flotilla of Pennsylvania Railroad heavyweight, six-axle horse cars—each one bearing, on its flanks, the name of a celebrated racing stable lettered in gilt against a Tuscan-red background— was put to other uses. To dissuade the many thousands of spectators who had been coming by train to New York or to Philadelphia for the yearly Army-Navy football game from making the journey, the match was booked for West Point one fall, and few outsiders could get to it. Putting on extra trains for summer and winter resorts was discontinued; so was the train that had run along one bank of the Thames, north of New London, Connecticut, for the Harvard-Yale crew race.

None of this was enough. An order went out from the ODT that any passenger train that filled less than 40 percent of its seats during its run would be discontinued after a specified date. Solitary passenger trains that had loafed down many a branch line at times that bore no relationship to the schedule of any other train at either end of the run disappeared, never to return. The Pullman Company had more than seven thousand cars, new or old, in viable condition; the Budd Company had in service—on the Santa Fe, the Seaboard, the Atlantic Coast Line, and some other railways—a sizable fleet of sleeping cars, all of them new. A reassignment took place.

Under ODT jurisdiction, the long-distance overnight passenger train sometimes diminished considerably in grandeur: day coaches that had already lived a long life on commuter runs began slipping into the consist; the dining car vanished; the sleeping cars, perhaps four or five in number, were replaced by lounge cars with a few bedrooms at one end; the lounge portions were filled, every seat, with passengers who would sit up overnight. Passenger cars whose air conditioning depended upon a plentiful supply of cakes of ice in hampers beneath the floor were now running hot; so were the cars whose air conditioning depended upon a supply of freon gas. And on many of the long-distance trains whose grandeur lingered, Traffic Control held blocks of reservations, in both Pullmans and day coaches, for moving the "casual" groups of military personnel and civilian personnel and civilian consultants, engineers, and technicians now working for the military. To keep track of these reservations, a Consolidated Ticket Office, a duplicate of the consolidated offices the railways had maintained in midtown Chicago and in downtown and midtown New York, was set up in Traffic Control.

But the diversions of passenger cars from civilian to military use were not enough. A conference in the Pentagon led to the design of a troop sleeping car, a troop kitchen car, and a hospital car, and these were turned out in quantity. The troop sleeper was maximum capacity—three tiers of bunks on each side of the center aisle—"no frills." Many servicemen, who often spent days on end in these vehicles, came to prefer the now-extinct tourist sleeping car—likewise no frills, but with only two tiers of bunks—though they were distinctly *not* in favor of the ruling that in these cars *two* servicemen, not one, were to be billeted in the lower berths. The jokes about lower berths, not all of them admirable, that this mode of life brought about survive to this day, and so do many of the cars themselves. (The military always wanted everything it bought to be constructed of the very best materials.) They survive, not especially well disguised, as maintenance-of-way bunk cars; some hospital cars for a while have enjoyed careers of greater grandeur as lounge cars or as piano-bar cars on the *Broadway Limited* and several other of Amtrak's principal trains.

By these expedients the American railways and their Iron Trail helped shorten and win the war. And when peace came, it occasioned such a redeployment and homeward surge of military personnel that the ODT issued what was for the railways its most decisive decree—what was termed "the 450-mile rule": all sleeping cars whose journeys took them less than 450 miles were to be withdrawn, on a specified day, from civilian service and assigned to the movement of troops. The businessmen whose enterprises were at the end of the war reconverting from military production to their peacetime activities were on the move, too, but often now without benefit of overnight sleeping cars. The railways tried to offer substitutes. The Pennsylvania Railroad inaugurated one train in lieu of its former triad of nighttime Pullman services from Pittsburgh, a bastion of the war effort, to New York. The new train was the 3:00 P.M. *Steel King,* which climbed up the Alleghenies and then down

them on the way to New York, as fast as a brace of the Pennsy's celebrated K-4 Pacifics could move it. It provided all the amenities from dining car to parlor cars to an observation car. The New Haven, its all-Pullman night train (*The Owl*) between Boston and New York shot from under it, tried to make do by replacing it with a string of parlor cars—a pillow and blanket for the occupant of every parlor-car seat on the night's run.

But while rail travel became more difficult for businessmen, other means of travel became more attractive. The military was now relaxing its hold on the huge allotment of airline seats it had commandeered; another arm of the government was relaxing its regulations on the use of gasoline, and the automobile came into its own again. The American businessman (or, at any rate, most of his kind) departed the rails—and forever. The railways had helped win one big war; now they were beginning to lose another.

Into the vale of Bethel charges Central Vermont Railway's robust 2-10-4 No. 701 (above), with international tonnage destined for the Canadian port of Montreal and eventually for our European allies. Opposite, above, through Green Mountain countryside as lush as Bethel's, sister 2-10-4 No. 703 and a lead consolidation span the Connecticut River heading another manifest toward the Canadian border. The ten 700-series 2-10-4's on the Central Vermont were built by American Locomotive in 1928 and now, in the forties, are New England's largest locomotives. Opposite, below, one of Boston & Maine's beautiful Mountains pounds downgrade on a westbound run through Williamstown, Massachusetts, her train richly mantled in a robe of coal smoke and flying dust. This is the busy 200-mile Fitchburg Division between Mechanicsville, New York, and the port of Boston, over which most of the railroad's war traffic flows toward the sea on its way to mysterious code destinations across the Atlantic. (COLLECTION, COLLECTION, COLLINS)

The Boston & Maine: *Line of The Minute Man*—and looking it! This spread offers a look at the B&M living up to its name, hauling men and material to and from the major naval yards at Boston and Portsmouth, and between the two big air bases it serves, Westover Field and Grenier Field. The B&M has been as closely identified with the war effort as Boston has been with baked beans. At right, the white flags are positioned on another of Uncle Sam's "specials," while below, a woman turntable operator lines the rails for big Berkshire No. 4015 at Mechanicsville, New York, B&M's western terminus and vital east-west interchange. This is the first time the Boston & Maine has employed women "out on the line" in the road's 117 years of existence. Opposite, above, the regular-carded *Green Mountain Flyer* gets out of Rutland, Vermont, under the boiling exhaust of pooled B&M P-3-a Pacific No. 3704 headed for Troy, New York, over Rutland rails. Opposite, below, one of B&M's beautiful dual-service Mountains, No. 4114 "Invincible," gives the boys in khaki a fast ride toward Boston and their waiting ships. School children along the line named twenty-eight of B&M's modern engines in a spirited contest. The 4113 (at right) was named the "Black Arrow." (HASTINGS, PICKETT, COLLECTION, COLLECTION)

That white scallop-shelled front opposite belongs to one of Boston & Albany's superpower A-1s Berkshires, shown taking on water at Beacon Park, Boston, before heading west over the 199 miles through the rugged Berkshire Mountains for which her type was named. The Boston & Albany, maintaining seventeen freight interchange points with four roads, hauled 527 tons of oil in 1939 and an incredible 1,599,828 tons in 1942, skirting Hitler's undersea wolf pack prowling off the eastern coast. The view at right is from the cab of 1426, as it teams up with sister No. 1421 leaving Beacon Park to pick up westbound merchandise. Below, the crew off a local freight looks over the *Southwestern Limited* slamming by behind one of B&A's twenty J-2 class Hudsons, of obvious New York Central lineage. (COLLECTION)

Here's a trainload of goods that will be felt in Berlin! Looking a little battle-weary, but hard-muscled, New Haven's brutish L class 2-10-2 No. 3234, opposite, digs in on the point of symbol BO-3 at West Hartford, Connecticut, bound for Maybrook, New York, and ultimately Brunswick, Maryland, on the Baltimore & Ohio. BO-3's cargo of war materials consists mostly of precision-engineered components for assembly-line production and of brass shell casings, both commodities to be shipped to war production plants throughout the country. Above, and certainly no less a brute than the 3234, a burly three-cylindered class R-3 Mountain rides the table at Cedar Hill, Connecticut, where she has been readied to forward New Haven's *Speed Witch* fast freight up the 156 miles to Boston. No. 3505 is rated for 5,500 tons on this run, and is equipped with automatic train-stop equipment used on the busy Shore Line Division. The vast Cedar Hill yards handle close to 9,500 cars daily on 154 miles of track! (COCHRANE, COLLECTION)

On December 7, 1941, at 7:50 A.M. (Hawaiian time), while 360 Japanese planes were attacking the U.S. fleet at Pearl Harbor, a new general-service Alco diesel was being introduced on the New Haven—a diesel that would soon become an important weapon of war on the home front. With a main line of 229 miles from New York to Boston, in one of the most highly industrialized and populated areas in America, the New Haven was confronted with a tremendous surge in both passenger and freight traffic. Rarely was any portion of its Shore Line quiet. New Haven's strategy was to employ its "streamlined giants" as daytime passenger-movers and nighttime freight-haulers.

Above, two of the dual-service Alco DL-109 diesels handle eastbound symbol OB-2 through the cut at Poughquag, New York. Opposite, above, one of the road's swift and handsome I-5 class Hudsons speeds the *Mayflower* eastward at Leete's Island, Connecticut. Opposite, below, class-L 2-10-2 No. 3210 walks a mile of empties around the curve at Beacon Falls, Connecticut, en route to Waterbury. She'll return on DN-1 to Cedar Hill, loaded with machined war parts made in the heavily industrialized Naugatuck valley. During the war, Waterbury was second only to Boston in total carloads in the New England states. (COCHRANE, COLLINS, DONAHUE)

37

Obviously, not all freight has been allocated to the war. New York Central, for example, delivers over twelve thousand carloads of livestock a year to Manhattan Island and the greater metropolitan area's ten million people. Four milk trains—one million gallons' worth—arrive in New York City *each day,* and over fifty cars of poultry, each car carrying 4,500 fowl, are delivered daily! From automobiles to mail and meat, Central's hot-footing trains deliver the goods to Gotham. Fast freight XN-2 (opposite, above) speeds meat and merchandise through the spans at Garrison, New York, toward New York City—L-3 Mohawk No. 3023 doing the honors. Opposite, below, with practically all other power out on the railroad, Central's streamlined Hudson No. 5451 is run through the washer at Harmon, New York, in preparation for the nightly run on the *20th Century Limited* to Chicago. Above, some "Rommel Routers" and other war goods arrive at Weehawken, New Jersey, and their port of embarkation. Each day this scene is repeated, as yards are filled and emptied with "gifts" for the Axis. Every day, freight cars carrying enough to feed over half the country's population for a day roll into the ports with food for export. At left, two high-drivered Pacifics have cut off their train and are heading up the engine lead at Harmon after substituting for a 4-8-2 on a merchandise run. Electrics take over for the rest of the run into New York City. (NOWAK, COLLECTION, COLLECTION, COLLECTION)

39

A closeup and a panoramic view give a feeling of what it was like to witness two Lehigh & New England engines raising hell—and hoppers—on the stiff grade eastbound at Summit, Pennsylvania. No ordinary backwoods operation here; consider, if you will: the big-boilered 2-8-0 and its mammoth 2-10-0 partner are teaming up, boosters cut in, with a whaling 189,320 pounds of combined tractive effort. Not often does *any* steam road come up with a power combo like this one! Oh yes—the coal-laden train is en route to Campbell Hall, New York, and an interchange with New Haven's Maybrook bridge route to New England. (COLLINS)

The fighting front of the Erie! The railroad that used the first iron rails made in the United States; over whose lines the first train order flashed; that laid the first six-foot-gauge rails, with incredibly wide clearances—the Erie is a formidable tool in Uncle Sam's arsenal, handling the big loads that the other eastern carriers can't accommodate. An ad that reached millions through newspapers and magazines showed the Army's huge new invasion barges in transit over the Erie. "Remember the man who built a boat in his basement? He's using it now from Suez to the Solomons," went the copy, citing the old story "about the man who built a boat in his basement and then couldn't get it out. Recently our Army and Navy and Marine Corps had a similar problem, but they found the answer, too." The Erie's broad, high clearances make it possible for huge weapons to be built along the railroad, hundreds of miles from the port of New York.

Below, two of Erie's towering 16'4"-high Berkshires double-head a hotshot west, rounding the curve at Hankins, New York, along the Delaware River. Erie obviously was balancing power, as SOP was to trust any train to just one of the 105 big Berks. At left, Erie's N1 class 2-8-2 No. 3075 tramps out of Conneaut Lake, Pennsylvania, with GI's, from the nearby camp, bound for New York and the crossing to Europe. The extra is heading out on the rails of the Bessemer & Lake Erie. Opposite, big Lima S-2 No. 3323 leans into the curve at Millrift, Pennsylvania, four miles out of Port Jervis, New York, her mile of train still in New York State. (LEWIS, COLLINS, COLLINS)

The classic 4-8-2 Mountain-type wheel arrangement was first widely used by the Boston & Maine, the first five models going into service in early 1935. The railroad stayed with a good thing; five more Mountain types were delivered to the B&M in 1936, followed by an additional three in 1940. During the early months of 1941, Baldwin delivered to the B&M five more "super models," each sporting fourteen-wheel centipede tanks and having roller bearings on all axles. These 73″-drivered machines were considered the ultimate in their wheel arrangement, having the latest "state-of-the-art" improvements.

Bridge-route Lehigh & Hudson River tried out several Lackawanna 1400-series 4-8-2's over their ninety-six-mile, moderate-graded line in the late thirties and found them well suited to their operating needs. During the war, when the little road's "shortcut route to New England" became a proverbial steel highway and their brawny 2-8-0's and 2-8-2's weren't making the time management wanted to see, a decision was made to purchase high-speed 4-8-2's that could cover ground and work tonnage. Under War Production Board restrictions, an exisiting design had to be used, and the road settled on Boston & Maine's beautiful R-1d. This spread shows three L&HR westbound symbols: above, crossing the New York, Ontario & Western at Burnside, New York; opposite, above, between McAfee, New Jersey, and Hamburg, New York; and opposite, below, leaving Maybrook, New York. (COLLINS)

By the time hostilities—and war traffic—involved the United States, the diesel had gotten its snout into the roundhouse door. B&O planners kept a close watch on diesel development, not letting the line's coal traffic influence their thinking. Realizing that road passenger diesels would eliminate the two, and sometime three, engine changes on the *Capitol Limited*'s 767-mile run between Washington and Chicago, the B&O in 1937 placed orders with General Motors' Electro Motive Division (EMD) for six 3,600-horsepower A-B tandem units. These units were regarded as the first true "off-the-shelf" production-line passenger diesels. Opposite, No. 51, the first of the order, along with a B and another A unit, rumbles across Thomas Viaduct heading the eastbound *Ambassador* in the summer of '44.

B&O's president, Daniel Willard, an ex-locomotive engineer, and Willard's pioneering motive-power developer, George Emerson, were always concerned first and foremost with a train's head end. Both were indefatigable in their desire to use the latest proven motive power available and it was no secret that they were infatuated with the new sleek diesels on their railroad. They were certainly not alone: total unfilled U.S. railroad orders for diesel locomotives in 1941 amounted to 450,000 horsepower; in 1942, the figure rose to 830,000 h.p., leaping to 1,170,000 h.p. by 1943!

The B&O badly needed freight power for the war effort and the War Production Board ordered the road to stick with steam. Thirty big, beautiful EM-1 class 2-8-8-4's—the biggest B&O could handle—were ordered from Baldwin in 1943. Once these giants went to work on the property, there were no regrets over not being able to get freight diesels! Below, one-month-old EM-1 No. 7611 gets a roll on *St. Louis-97* downgrade through Terra Alta, West Virginia. (COLLECTION, GALLAGHER)

Even during the war, if time-on-the-run is available—and, of course, manpower—Southern likes to hose down engines with an 80-degree mixture of oil and water, under pressure. If more time is available, the green jacket will get wiped down. Such has been the case with Southern's trim Pacific No. 1215 (opposite), taking on sand at Potomac yard, outside of Washington, D.C. Above, yard personnel get their first look at a spanking-new Atlantic Coast Line EMD freighter that was run through on a test over the RF&P from Potomac yard to Richmond. The vast Potomac yard is the interchange between the Baltimore & Ohio and the Pennsylvania railroads on the north and the Chesapeake & Ohio, the Richmond, Fredericksburg & Potomac, and the Southern Railway on the south. In 1943, loaded or empty cars totaling 1,422,244 were cleared through the yard, an increase of 96 percent over prewar 1940. The peak month was May 1943, when 266,166 cars were handled—the maximum for a single day was 5,092 cars! At left, a well-maintained Chesapeake & Ohio Northern heads out of Clifton Forge, Virginia, for a main-train assignment. (RONFOR, COLLECTION, KERRIGAN)

49

The call to the defense of the nation has brought a solid front of seemingly endless coal trains rumbling out of the deep hills of West Virginia, down to the docks and waiting ships on the tidewater. Coal! The commodity that generates well over half of our nation's electricity, that is the base for over 85 percent of our plastics and 100 percent of the steel for our weapons of war, is moving on a priority basis, rolling on a boulevard of steel. At left, three Virginian EL3A motors thunder onto the bridge at Bud, West Virginia, doing their part by moving the procession of empties back to the mines. Below, a quartet of Norfolk & Western LC2 class motors clank along under the 11,000-volt AC, moving the loads eastward through Powhatan, West Virginia. Contrary to what the picture suggests, the Norfolk & Western is typically the story of its 310 modern steamers storming along a manicured 131-pound main, towing pure low-volatile coal of the highest quality. In the West Virginia countryside between Eckman and Bluefield, however, where tunnels present gas problems for steam, these slow-moving, powerful electrics take over, eliminating the need for double-heading steamers—and crews.

Opposite, one of Virginian's huge AG mallets moves down the main, like a sweating Goliath! BA No. 215 waits comfortably out of the way on the 7,600-foot siding at Suffern, Virginia, for the big 900 and her 13,000-ton, 175-car train to pass. Virginian, like neighbor Norfolk & Western, has the same basic straight-shot run, from mine to tidewater. (COOK, COOK, COLLECTION)

To move an infantry division of fifteen thousand men and their equipment, sixty-five trains—totaling 1,350 cars—are required! The handsome pair of Southern Mikes opposite, backing through the yard at Chattanooga late on an August day in 1942, will pick up one of the many extras that have been required to move an infantry division from nearby Fort Oglethorpe. Practically all of Southern's fast freights handle highly remunerative war supplies, such as munitions, with freight revenue per car averaging a record ninety dollars.

At right, one of Florida East Coast's regal Mountains blasts the sunny skies, stepping out of Jacksonville with the third section of the *Florida Special*—while the folks in the "10-1-2" sleeper get an earful of stack talk through the ventilators! During the war-year winter seasons, Jacksonville was one of the busiest rail towns in America, constantly jammed to capacity with regular and extra vacation trains, along with the military traffic.

Below, one of Nashville, Chattanooga & St. Louis's light J1C Mountains arrives in Chattanooga after running the curving, almost corkscrewlike 134 miles of track from Atlanta. New power will be put on the train for the remaining 151 miles to Nashville. The railroad was built with as many curves per mile as any main-line stretch of track in America in order to hold the ruling grade to 0.7 percent through mountainous country. Typical of conditions on the run over from Atlanta is the section of track that staggers through 13 miles of tight curves connecting points just 2½ miles apart, due east of Marietta, Georgia, home of the Bell Aircraft plant and Uncle Sam's newest weapon, the B-29. The presence of No. 561 and the other Mountain types on the NC&StL roster is the result of an order by the United States Railroad Administration during World War I to replace the 4-6-2's with 4-8-2's, which could better handle the heavy troop and wartime freight trains over the "Lookout Mountain Route" between Atlanta and Nashville.

(PALMER, LAVAKE, PALMER)

Saluda grade on the Southern's Asheville Division is the crookedest and steepest standard-gauge main line in the United States. For three miles on the westbound haul, the grade varies from 4.09 to 4.7 percent—steep enough to force a mighty 2-10-2, possessed of 74,000 pounds of tractive effort, "down on her knees" with a meager 500 tons, exclusive of tender and caboose, behind her drawbar. An articulated 2-8-8-2 with 96,000 pounds of tractive effort can handle only 50 tons more than a 2-10-2, and pretty soon we start worrying about drawbars! Opposite, one of Southern's gargantuan Ss class 2-10-2's, affectionately called a "fifty" by those who run 'em, throws its massive weight against the rails at the base of Saluda's 4.7 percent, with tonnage bound for Asheville, North Carolina. In a few moments, all momentum will be lost on the initial 4.7-percent and longer 4.4-percent grades; the 2-10-2's—one fore, one aft, working together and wide open—will fight every inch of grade through the Blue Ridge Mountains, into the "land of the sky."

Crowd pleaser? At left, a new FT diesel freight locomotive noses in among the well-polished Southern steam power at Monroe, Virginia. The War Production Board has allocated all freight diesel production to EMD; Alco and Baldwin are restricted to building diesel switching units, along with steam engines.

Below, the dog days of summer and a breather from war duty: Seaboard's dogged R-1 2-6-6-4—a doggerel beast—lays over at Atlanta prior to returning to Raleigh. Not to be dogmatic about it, I feel that this picture comes close to substantiating the widely held opinion that the eight SAL 82,300-pound-tractive-effort 2-6-6-4 articulateds were for the dogs! (DONAHUE, COLLECTION, COLLECTION)

Within a few months of the United States' entry into the war, most of the railroads had to revise their operations drastically in order to meet the ever-growing and ever-changing demands made upon them by the military. For the Appalachian coal carriers, the demand for coal multiplied threefold overnight and the roads found themselves in a veritable maelstrom of coal traffic—loads and empties, coming and going, in all directions at once!

Fortunately, for the most part the coal roads were ready for whatever Uncle Sam demanded, all having made huge investments in rolling stock, track, and port facilities prior to the war. *If* there was any inherent weakness, it was in

the ranks of older motive power, but all the coal roads immediately undertook massive rebuilding programs, while at the same time placing orders for new power. By the end of the first quarter of 1942, the major coal roads, without exception, were setting new records for operating efficiency, thus contributing their share to the national war effort.

Pictured on this spread is the timeless story of men against mountains. With exhausts roaring, stoker feeds going, and firemen hoping their fires won't be torn up by the heavy exhausts—or by an engine slipping—two B&O mallet compound 2-8-8-0's shake heaven and earth in a show of savage fury, lending their all in getting another coal train up the steel over Cranberry grade in the Alleghenies. Below, one of the road's new and beautiful Baldwin EM-1 simple articulateds drifts through Salt Lick curve in West Virginia—downgrade toward M&K Junction, Nowlesburg, and eventually Grafton—after having crested Seventeen-Mile grade and its average 2.18 percent. The smoke from helpers 7040 and 7038 has cleared, but the sand-covered roadbed always attests to the tortuous climb for the eastbounds at this point. (COLLECTION)

Inside the cab (opposite), everything's shaking, the water dances in the glass at the three-quarter mark, the deck plate slams and bangs, stoker screw grinds, gauges jiggle, steam sputters and spits from backhead pipes, the fire roars, and the veteran fireman leans way out to look at his stack. Steam gauges register a steady 218 pounds. The younger fireman on the road engine does the same, things looking as though he's overcrowding his fire. The lead engine heaves and hunts; rods pound rhythmically as the two "Big Sixes" blast upgrade through Cumberland Narrows, while the crashing echoes of booming stacks hammer hard off the rocks. Steadily *Second Chicago-97* makes progress along the Pittsburgh line. At left, big EM-1 No. 7603 pulls hard on famed Cranberry grade, west of Terra Alta, West Virginia. Below, two mallets create a little thunder—and shove—on the rear end of an oil train, moving a steady eight miles per hour up Cranberry's 2.2-percent ruling grade. B&O's motive power department likes to assign 350,000 pounds tractive effort *per train* over the Alleghenies! (DONAHUE, COLLECTION, COLLECTION)

Here is a look at the railroad that carries more freight and more passengers than any other railroad during the war. Although it has neither the greatest rail mileage nor the greatest geographic spread, the Pennsylvania Railroad serves the heart of the richest traffic-producing areas in the country. The Pennsy is the chief carrier of America's number-one war material, steel—and interestingly, the steel industry in fact grew out of the iron rail originally laid by the PRR. On these two pages, some of the trains that contributed to the 1.4 billion tons moved over the Pennsylvania Railroad between 1941 and 1945 are shown on and around the famed Horse Shoe curve in Altoona, Pennsylvania.

Above, two of the road's ponderous workhorse Decapods slog it out on the rear end of a munitions train, working the important and dangerous cargo up over the 92-foot-per-mile grade along the east slope of the Alleghenies. At right, a fast-running M-1 Mountain works preference freight train NL-1, the *Yankee,* around Horse Shoe curve, en route to Chicago with goods from New England. Opposite, above, another Mountain, No. 6743, cants around the main curve and onto a brief tangent, rolling hot stock train FW-8 downgrade in a haze of coal smoke and brakeshoe smoke. Opposite, below, the firemen lean way out—way out!—watching the 80″ drivers of their K-4's and the T-1 hitting the crossovers, getting a main train west, out of Altoona. In ten minutes, they'll be encountering Horse Shoe. (COLLECTION)

Wham! Bessemer & Lake Erie's great H1A Texas type No. 618 (opposite) pounds past with a solid train of the good red earth from the Iron Range that will go into making steel and the weapons of war. From the mile-long docks at Conneaut, Ohio, and along the 0.8 percent main of the B&LE, two of these great locomotives, employing their combined 216,470 pounds of booster-equipped tractive effort, easily move the immense 13,050-ton trains up Hog Back Hill and on to Albion (Pittsburgh). During the war, the B&LE acquired seventeen additional Texas types to assure the vital movement of ore.

At right, a common sight during the hectic traffic patterns of war: the Wabash stages a power-balancing move, highballing two ballast-scorching, dust-raising Mountain types and a hack near Montpelier, Ohio. Below, one of Chesapeake & Ohio's fabulous T-1 class 2-10-4's easily handles the standard 13,500-ton, 160-car coal train from Russell, Kentucky, to Toledo. At Toledo's great Presque Isle coal-loading terminal, the coal will be transferred into lake vessels for delivery over water to northern ports. (COLLECTION, COOK, COLLECTION)

Each one a weapon of war: the streamliner and the ore train. The streamliners went to war—in many ways. The pioneer streamliner, Union Pacific's three-car aluminum *City of Salina,* was scrapped and reclaimed for war materials, and the nation's newest trains took off the frills, added cars, and, in some cases, slowed down schedules to permit the handling of more GI's. While troop trains (or *main trains,* as they were called) moved the bulk of the companies and divisions, the nation's streamliners carried essential civilians, servicemen traveling independently, and sometimes small-scale troop movements of groups on special orders.

Below, New York Central's wartime *Empire State Express,* no longer the knight-in-armor she was on December 7, 1941, now carries extra cars in her role as tireless workhorse. She's shown rushing east through Euclid, Ohio, on April 11, 1943. Opposite, Pennsy's big, ponderous N-1-s class 2-10-2 No. 9226 is about to clank across Wheeling & Lake Erie's main south of Cleveland, with iron ore for the hungry mills in and around Pittsburgh. The rich red ore of Minnesota, the white stone of Pennsylvania, and the black rock of West Virginia will all travel by rail to the same mills; out of them will emerge more grim guardians of our cherished liberty. (COOK)

Across the board—every American railroad has its glowing accounts of the preparations and operations that made it possible to handle the unprecedented volume of war traffic. "The Old Reliable"—Louisville & Nashville, to strangers—took great pride in the fact that prior to Pearl Harbor the railroad had put its house in order by reducing the number of bad-order cars and locomotives to the bare minimum. Before the U.S. involvement in the war, the L&N undertook a tremendous rebuilding and modernization program for their newest steam locomotives, and at the same time commenced a tremendously ambitious program to upgrade all main-line track. Early in 1941, after getting by with nothing larger than a 2-8-2, the road ordered fourteen of the heaviest and most modern 2-8-4's money could buy. Twelve diesel switchers and eight sleek 4,000-h.p. diesel passenger locomotives were also ordered (ironically, the passenger diesels were ordered so that steam could be released to handle "more important duties," according to a news release!). Above, two of the road's new E-6 passenger diesels rumble past HK Tower at Anchorage, Kentucky, with the southbound *Pan-American.* Lightweight coaches had been ordered from ACF to go with the diesels but could not be delivered during the war—thus the standard equipment.

Opposite, above, and a powerful example of the ultimate in steam locomotive design, Pennsy's huge, 8,000-h.p. Q-2 No. 6131 thunders east out of Englewood, Illinois, with its wartime payload of 150 high cars. No. 6131 was built at Altoona in August 1944; a total of twenty-six Q-2's would ultimately be built.

Opposite, below, some traditional railroading as we like to see it! L&N's graceful L-1 Mountain No. 402 departs Cincinnati with Second #17, the *Flamingo,* en route to Atlanta and ultimately to Florida. Pennsy's northbound *South Land* is seen arriving on the adjacent track. The heavy first section of the *Flamingo* is regularly handled by one of L&N's big freight-hauling M-1 class Berkshires equipped with steam heat; a second section usually draws a class L-1. From 1939 to 1944 passenger business increased 400 percent on the Old Reliable. One note about that beautiful 402: she's the classic example (without L&N's traditional oversized headlight) of the basic 4-8-2 designed for the United States Railway Administration during the First World War. Opinion is almost unanimous that the basic USRA designs for steam locomotives came close to aesthetic perfection. (COLLECTION)

Throughout the war, the New York Central saw to it that its prestigious *20th Century Limited* continued to maintain the high standards for which the train was known. The extra fare charge of $7.50 was reduced to $5.00 (same as for the *Broadway Limited*) to assure constant capacity loads. No cars were added, nor was the schedule lengthened to handle extra troops; a valet was "stationed" in one end of the crew-dormitory car and a secretary in the other end of the same car, in a lounge. In company advertisements, both the valet and secretary were pictured in a cutaway drawing of the car, "ready to handle important war errands," from the pressing of uniforms to the typing of military drafts and letters. In ads, both the New York Central and Pullman conductors were referred to as "ticket teams," the dining-car steward was called the "commissary commander," and the ever-on-guard rear brakeman was depicted as the train's "rear guard"! Military clichés aside, the *Century* was an important train for military personnel—and always a magnificent sight arriving at the end of its New York–Chicago run.

68

In 1944, the New York Central carried over twenty-four million passengers over its Western Division and Michigan Central West Division into Chicago. On the average, 284 cars were serviced *each day* in Central's Root Street coach yard—not including the 35 to 40 dining cars stocked and serviced daily! For lovers of satistics: the number of meals served in New York Central dining cars operating out of Chicago during 1944 was 2,379,858, compared to the more normal 856,110 meals served in 1940. In 1944 alone, Cen-

tral moved over a million carloads of war matériel over its MC West and Western divisions. Above, one of New York Central's classic Hudsons rumbles across the Wabash River at Lafayette, Indiana, with the Chicago-to-Cincinnati *Queen City Special* in tow. This train and its opposite-direction counterpart, the *Sycamore*, offered the fastest wartime schedule over the 303-mile route between the two cities and carried through-cars of the C&O, for service to and from Washington, D.C. (NOWAK, NOWAK, COOK)

Perhaps the most heated passenger-train competition during the war was to be found between Chicago and Milwaukee, on the steel raceways of the Milwaukee Road and Chicago & North Western. In 1941, the Milwaukee had twenty-five trains on this run, while rival North Western dispatched twenty-one—all ballast-scorchers. Both railroads carded their hottest trains over the 85-mile run on a flat 75-minute schedule. Above, an 84″-drivered F-7 Hudson limbers up, near the century mark, on a second section of Milwaukee Road's northbound *Morning Hiawatha* through Rondout, Illinois, not too far from the celebrated curve at Deerfield clearly posted REDUCE TO 90.

Opposite, Milwaukee Road's burly S-2 class 4-8-4 No. 208

marches merchandise through the vast Armour estate in West Lake Forest, Illinois, en route to the Chicagoland yards at Bensenville. When called upon, this big fellow can easily handle the eighteen-car *Olympian* over the 915 undulating miles between Minneapolis and Harlowton, Montana, as well as numerous troop trains. As fast-freight haulers, the 4-8-4's replaced seventy older Mikados and quickly showed engine crews, shippers, and dispatchers what a 74″-drivered Northern could do in a little time! In 1937, when No. 208 was built, attempts to pretty up the iron horse were well under way, and there was much talk of reducing head-on air resistance by reducing clutter. The Milwaukee obviously wasn't listening! (KERRIGAN)

In this sequence, Burlington's *Twin Cities Zephyr* waits on the wye track for a troop train to clear. The great 0-5 class 4-8-4 No. 5621 heading the long main train was the first of a final batch of modern dual-service Northerns built by the railroad in 1938, two years after the *Zephyr.* The big dual-service Northerns and other newer locomotives made up only 30 percent of the Burlington's motive power, but they performed from 45 to 60 percent of the road work during the war years—and this situation was repeated on most of the railroads.

With the troop train now in the clear, "Pegasus," the power car on the *Zephyr,* backs the beautiful train up into the wye (opposite) as the rear-end brakeman gives hand signals from the lowered step of parlor-obs car "Jupiter." Each car on the two fluted stainless-steel *Twin Zephyr*s, (as they are collectively called) is named after a classical god or goddess, and the trains are commonly referred to as the "Trains of the Gods and Goddesses." Both *Zephyr*s were designed and built by Budd in 1936 as seven-car articulated trains. Within six months of their initial run, the increased patronage of the popular trains demanded the addition of an eighth car to each. It is no secret that modern light-weight trains, through higher-speed operation, are doing more than their share in increasing the railroad's passenger capacity. Running on tight schedules, the streamliners are depended on for both military and essential civilian traffic. The sixteen cars of the two *Twin Cities Zephyr*s run 882 miles a day. (COLLECTION)

One-half mile east of St. Paul Union Depot—out by the roundhouse and overlooking the maze of wye tracks—is perhaps the best "train-parade reviewing stand" in America! All eight railroads serving St. Paul jointly own the Union Depot and its twenty-one platform tracks. Confusing as it may sound, most trains leave eastward to go west to Minneapolis, wyeing to the northeast and passing southward, by the "reviewing stand," twice—when they arrive and when they depart. Above, and at right, Burlington's gleaming *Twin Cities Zephyr* heads into St. Paul after wyeing. Opposite, Burlington's conventional train #52 and Chicago & North Western's regal diesel-powered *400* depart St. Paul, each in its own distinctive way. (COLLECTION)

74

A few minutes after the *Twin Cities Zephyr* has headed into the station, stout Colorado & Southern Mike No. 803, leased to the Burlington, appears (above), working a cut of fifty-seven cars over from Great Northern's Cedar Lake yard. With a loud, clear exhaust, the 2-8-2 will boom under the Roberts Street Bridge and continue on past "Pegasus" and her waiting train, out to the Q's own yard.

Opposite, the 5621 has wyed and now backs its heavy consist of troop sleepers and standard Pullmans past the roundhouse and ready tracks and into the St. Paul station. The Northern Pacific A-5 class Northern is ready for her next assignment and steams alone, where only minutes ago, a sister A-5 and a W-3 class Mike were laying over, waiting to pick up their trains. (COLLECTION)

Today's ore in the vast Mesabi Range in Minnesota will be tomorrow's battleships, tanks, shot and shells. Mother Earth, with her rich bounty, sustains mankind, but now the great open-pit mines of Mother Earth—and northern Minnesota—are spawning the weapons to destroy mankind. The huge Mesabi Iron Range, America's steel backbone, contributed more than 1.5 billion tons of high-grade ore to help win World War I; now, in World War II, the herculean engines and trains of the Duluth, Mesabi & Iron Range Railroad mother still more of the precious red ore on its way down to the docks on Lake Superior and the waiting ore boats. Pictured here are three great DM&IR locomotives leading their parade of ore jennies to and from the docks at Duluth and Two Harbors: a 2-8-8-2 class M-2-S

mallet (opposite, below), and two magnificent class M Yellowstone 2-8-8-4's (below and opposite above). The M-2-S No. 210 was orginally built, in 1917, as a compound mallet designed to walk fifty-five jennies plus caboose up the 2.2 percent Proctor grade at a steady 11.75 miles an hour. In 1929, she was rebuilt into a faster, more powerful simple articulated. As for the Yellowstones—they were among the world's most powerful locomotives and were ordered from Baldwin to help with the tremendous wartime iron ore traffic. They exceeded all performance expectations, steamed beautifully, rode like Pullmans, and were loved by their crews. During 1942, 44,788,199 tons of ore were dragged out of the hills and down to the docks by the ranks of DM&IR engines. (PICKETT, COLLINS, PICKETT)

Putting the heat on Hitler! Opposite, a brawny Chicago & North Western class H-1 4-8-4 appears impatient, waiting at the Nelson, Illinois, chute for the crashing flow of black diamonds into its tender. No. 3016's crew, resting upon 76″ drivers and having 84,200 pounds of tractive effort to work with, will waste no time moving the solid meat block eastward across the flat Illinois countryside to Chicago. In 1929, when the class H engines were built, the C&NW understandably touted them as "the largest dual-service locomotives in the world."

Above, Santa Fe's recently shopped Mike No. 3287 leads a westbound war extra through Willow Springs, Illinois, under a billowing trail of steam. At left, Milwaukee's husky 4-8-4 No. 224 works a priority train across a bleak, wintry South Dakota landscape, en route to the port of Seattle. The battle cry "Engines on the warpath!" could describe the locomotives pictured here—and throughout this book. (KERRIGAN, DELANO, DELANO)

On August 20, 1942, upon the occasion of Missouri Pacific's Sedalia shops completing the last of twenty-five "Victory Locomotives"—all rebuilt from 63"-drivered 2-8-4's into roller-bearing 75"-drivered 4-8-4's—Missouri Governor F. C. Donnell sent a wire to the 1,100 shopmen on the project, paying "tribute to this Victory Locomotive [No. 2125, the final rebuild] and to the railroad employees throughout our nation for the constant and vital services they are rendering." Although that twenty-fifth Victory Locomotive is not pictured, here is a look at the Missouri Pacific at war.

Opposite, MOP's beautiful N-73 class Northern No. 2211 (ordered from Baldwin one year after the completion of No. 2125) waits in the hole at California, Missouri, her pops lifting into the sultry summer air. Above, No. 2211 is pictured on another day, as road engine on a redball west, raising the dust near the town of California. It is doubtful whether the small-drivered Consol is helping 2211's forward progress! At left, one of Missouri Pacific's magnificently proportioned 2-8-2's works some "black gold" and general merchandise across the bridge at Little Rock, Arkansas. (COLLECTION)

The Frisco has taken bold, unprecedented steps to tell us we're at war—on the home front. In a constant barrage of ads aimed at the general public and in direct mailings to their customers and shippers, Frisco has made it clear that Uncle Sam comes first along the iron trail. *The government has first call on all equipment for the movement of men and matériel. Your interests, whether passenger or shipper, are secondary.* To some sixteen thousand shippers and prospects, and to over thirty-three thousand frequent travelers located along the Frisco routes, go patriotic mailings every month, assuring them: "Come what may—and whatever the need—Frisco is prepared to keep 'em rolling." Employees all over the line, accustomed to seeing the FRISCO FIRST slogan on banners and signs now see FRISCO crossed off and *U.S.A.* superimposed. The message is clear.

Some behind-the-scenes shots of the Frisco: Opposite, above, the Tulsa call boy at the crew dispatcher's office chalks up a crew for the "Tulsa switcher" between phone calls to road crews. A quick glance at the board indicates the road's big new 4500 class Northerns have been delivered and are working the war-swollen Eastern Division along with the road's thirty-four heavy and twenty medium 4300 and 4400 class Mountains. The big 4100 class Mikes have relieved many consolidations and are doing yeoman service on the flatter western lines of the Frisco. Spick-and-span Frisco keeps an engine washer round the clock; opposite, below, a hostler runs the big Mike past the detergent gun. On this page: the crew on the 4103. They will soon head out to the departure yard to take over on the head end of hotshot #438. (DELANO)

The Southwest became a hive of transportation activity following Pearl Harbor. The numerous camps, training schools, and other military establishments increased inbound and outbound traffic beyond anything that could have been expected. On January 17, 1942, news that the huge tanker *ESSO Allen Jackson* had been torpedoed off the coast of Hatteras quickly spread throughout the nation. America was stunned. During the next six months, 506 U.S. ships, totaling three million tons, were sunk (in comparison to only 21 Nazi U-boats)! The War Production Board issued the "Certificate of Necessity for Priority Action No. 1," which in essence established the movement of oil by rail as the highest priority in domestic transportation. Overnight, it was decided that the huge volume of oil that usually moved by ocean tanker to the East Coast would now move by rail. Oil for our forces, our allies, our industries, our homes—hundreds of thousands of barrels *each day*—was soon moving by train in every available tank car, in synthetic rubber tanks in boxcars, in oil drums, in converted gondolas—in *anything* that would hold the black gold! By mid-1943, the railroads were hauling over 900,000 barrels of oil to the Atlantic Seaboard each day. Once more, the impossible was accomplished.

Opposite—and typical of any southwestern rail hub—tank cars are classified into solid trainloads in Southern Pacific's yard at Beaumont, Texas. At right, a portrait of one of Frisco's beautiful thoroughbreds, Mountain type No. 1500. To many, these black-and-gold 4-8-2's, with their bluish jackets of Russian iron, were the most beautiful steam locomotives in the world. Below, the brakeman atop the tender of Texas & Pacific No. 616 takes careful aim with an orange—his target is the cab of 4-8-2 No. 901, waiting in the Dallas station with the *Southerner!* (PRINT COLLECTION, COLLECTION, COLLECTION)

The wartime demands made on the nation's railroads cannot be better illustrated than with the statistics of the medium-size Missouri-Kansas-Texas Railroad. In 1944, the average traffic density for the MKT was 2,407,300 ton-miles per mile of railroad—over 10 percent more than in 1943, 46 percent more than in 1942, and *172 percent* more than in 1941! The increase in tonnage and traffic density on the Katy main line was, with few exceptions, greater than on most other single-track railroads. The Katy, working with nothing larger than 4-6-2's and 2-8-2's, attained a daily average of 173.4 miles for their freights, compared to the national average of 125 miles. With good reason, the company publicly boasted about its high standards of mechanical practice.

Above, two spotless Katy Pacifics burnish the rails with a troop train at Temple, Texas, while at left, one of these stylish engines easily handles the northbound *Katy Flyer* near Denison, Texas. Opposite, Texas & Pacific's mighty 2-10-4 No. 663 urges a westbound extra into momentum out of Mineola, Texas. Of all the locomotives in America, the Texas & Pacific's fearsome-looking, pipe-laden 2-10-4's symbolized, to me, the nation's railroad muscle most graphically. Had Hitler had a poster of this brute on a wall somewhere, he might have had second thoughts! (PLUMMER)

The Katy is pictured again on this page, and typically Katy it is: a modestly proportioned 2-8-2, trimmed in white, with the scarlet KATY herald ornamenting its polished tender. Katy was a line without 4-8-4's and stainless-steel streamliners; it was a line of olive-green heavyweight varnish and first-line redballs, operated in the grandest and proudest tradition—a railroad that *could* be called "The Standard Railroad," right up until the diesel onslaught. No. 844 is shown here arriving at Fate, Texas, under a bluebonnet sky as the hogger keeps the slack taut and the head-end brakeman drops down to make a cut.

Cotton Belt, like Katy, is as much a part of Texas as hominy and grits. Across Arkansas and through the Ozarks, Cotton Belt, like the Katy, is a gateway carrier

into St. Louis. Cotton Belt is a road of fast freights, including the famed "Blue Streak" merchandiser. In 1935, the road petitioned for reorganization. When the war—and increased traffic—came, all accumulated interest was paid off; 112-pound rail was laid, replacing 665 miles of light rail, and centralized traffic control was installed on 191 miles of single track. Ten big 4-8-4's like No. 815—shown opposite, below, rolling a westbound hotshot through Texarkana, Texas—were built in the road's own Pine Bluff, Arkansas, shops; these were supplemented by ten others ordered from Baldwin. Opposite, above, Cotton Belt's only passenger train departs Sulphur Springs, Texas, behind a modest ten-wheeler. (PLUMMER)

Countless books have been written about the steam locomotive. Many classes have been singularly sighted for their aesthetic appeal, and, indeed, certain wheel arrangements are generally considered more handsome than others; sometimes one railroad's version in a particular class is unanimously accepted as the best-looking, but there is often disagreement. There are proponents of the clean and classic "USRA school," for whom simplicity of design rules; there are others who prefer the big, modern, powerful 4-8-4's, articulateds and the like, and who cultivate this breed as representative of the finest design in steam locomotion. All these have their admirers—but what roundhouse during the war held more magnificent machines than the house at Texarkana—the home for many an iron soldier of the Missouri Pacific and Texas & Pacific? Both roads offered a beautiful compromise, from the well-proportioned, strong, regal grace of Missouri Pacific, to the "well-hung" man-appeal of T&P's great roster. If I had to choose just *one* roundhouse to relish, I'd be walking the ranks at Texarkana! (PLUMMER)

Certainly little can be said about Union Pacific's Big Boys that isn't already known: They were the world's biggest, heaviest steam locomotives, built by American Locomotive Company in 1944, and named by the workmen who built them. The only 4-8-8-4's ever built, they were designed to handle the maximum tonnage drawbars would safely stand, at speed, over the Wyoming and Utah mountains. A Big Boy could run at eighty miles an hour—its running gear was designed to have great flexibility on curves and at the same time provide for relatively high rigidity when on tangent track Maximum power output could be continuously maintained at seventy miles per hour—a fabulous, even graceful, 1,197,800-pound machine. Big Boy could run, lug, and storm!

The bulk of Big Boy is evident in the above view of No. 4005 drifting through Green River, Wyoming, against the rugged escarpment of Independence Rock. Possessed of the longest-in-the-world wheelbase (132'9⅝"), these titans are used only between Cheyenne, Wyoming, and Ogden, Utah, where newly installed turntables can (barely) accommodate them. At left, a magnificent Big Boy sweats, sands, *storms* steadily up the long climb near Rock River, amid the endless panorama of flat, desolate, upland Wyoming country. Opposite, pictured in the glorious light of sunrise, Big Boy No. 4021 thunders east through Unitah, Utah, with a mile of freezers tagging behind. (GRIFFITHS, COLLINS, COLLINS)

By mid-1943, the war in the Pacific was raging and tonnage heading for West Coast ports was reaching astronomical figures. The Santa Fe took on the brunt of this traffic and was additionally burdened with a war of its own: it had to haul in millions of gallons of water to quench the thirst of its hard-working steam locomotives on desert and mountain divisions where local water was unavailable. This called for hundreds of tank cars. The situation was further aggravated on helper districts, where terrain prohibited additional track for tank car storage. And the more freight the locomotives hauled, the more water they needed!

From September 1942 until May 1943, Electro Motive had suspended diesel locomotive production because certain alloys needed for critical engine parts were in short supply. Although the Santa Fe possessed a stable of great modern steam locomotives, they clearly saw the need for diesels at this time.

In May 1943, the government saw to it that the necessary alloys were made available to EMD, and the Santa Fe was given first crack at an order. Sixty-eight four-unit 5,400-h.p. freight diesels were immediately ordered, to replace all steam locomotives in freight service between Winslow, Arizona, and Barstow, California. The new FT freighters performed yeoman service, handling 3,500-ton trains over mountains and across desert (versus steam's 2,000-ton average), and eliminating all helper service along the 459-mile route with the exception of one 23-mile stretch. On these pages, Santa Fe's FT set No. 115, after a brief mechanical inspection, heads out of the Winslow roundhouse to do battle. The emptiness of the house attests to the tremendous volume of traffic out on the railroad.

The diesels eliminated the bottleneck and broke Santa Fe traffic records. On November 28, 1944, no fewer than twenty-six westbound freights and twenty-one eastbound freights rolled through Winslow. On that same day, twenty passenger trains went through town! (DELANO)

On June 7, 1945, President Truman wrote J. M. Johnson, Director of the Office of Defense Transportation, that the railroads of the nation were now going to undertake "the most gigantic task in all the history of transportation"—moving the American armies "from the victorious battlefields of Europe to meet and wipe out the tyranny of the East." To do this job, "most of our soldiers will be transported the full length of the American continent."

In an efficient, quiet, and businesslike way, the railroads continued doing the impossible, in an impossibly short span of time. While General MacArthur's forces mopped up in the Philippines, the Marines were capturing Iwo Jima to give the B-29's based in the Marianas both fighter cover and a midway emergency field. With long-range fighter support, the B-29's could start to work on Japan.

As invasion plans were taking shape, down through California's Cajon Pass on the Santa Fe and the Union Pacific came more main trains than ever before—off the Pennsy and the New Haven, the New York Central and the Illinois Central—cars from every line in the country. Opposite, above, a 3800 class 2-10-2, still wearing its antiaircraft headlight shield, beats through Cajon with a munitions train; opposite, below, thirty cars of GI's drift down Cajon behind an immaculate 2-10-2; while at right, one of Southern Pacific's unique and powerful cab-in-front articulateds moves train #60, the *West Coast*, upgrade one mile east of Newhall, California. Given the SP's strategic location on the Pacific Coast, the War Production Board quickly approved orders in March 1941 for 40 additional 4-8-8-2's to supplement the 105 already in service. Another 50 followed during the balance of the war years. Below, the yard crew and one of Santa Fe's 1,000-h.p. Alco diesel switchers are shown at work in Los Angeles. (DELANO, COLLECTION, KELSO, DELANO)

The Pacific theater's greatest amphibious operation was the Allied landing on Okinawa—183,000 troops and 747,000 tons of cargo, using 430 assault transports and landing ships from 11 ports. Over a 53-day period, the American advance averaged a scant 133 yards a day, with casualties mounting to the highest number in the Pacific war. On June 21, 1945, Okinawa was secure. The way to Japan was now open. Major General Curtis LeMay's XXI Bomber Command, comprising nearly 1,000 B-29's, went to work over Yokohama, Nagoya, Tokyo, and Osaka. Sixty-six Japanese cities were hit by the Superfortresses; 485 of the big bombers were downed, 2,707 more damaged, and 3,041 of our flyers killed. For America, and for Japan, the end of a dreaded world war was near.

On September 2, 1945, the formal surrender documents officially ending the Second World War were signed aboard the battleship *Missouri* in Tokyo Bay. For the railroads, the unbelievable task of bringing the boys home began. In November, over 1,300,000 troops rode the trains home from their ports of arrival, and even more came home over the rails in December and January! This spread features two of the most heavily "troop-traveled" trains: Opposite, Union Pacific's racy Mountain No. 7869 heads into Los Angeles past Mission Tower with the newly refurbished *Los Angeles Limited*. Above, Southern Pacific's heavy *Sunset Limited* departs Los Angeles behind the formidable duo of Mountain No. 4334 and Daylight No. 4449. (KELSO)

2

THE
HOME
FRONT

THE MOST POWERFUL WEAPON the railways of the United States had at the ready to bring to bear in the Second World War was the steam locomotive. The rush of wartime traffic would delay its demise, although the diesel was already on the way up. The Union Pacific and the Santa Fe and the Southern Pacific and the Burlington steam engines that had hauled the best of the fast trains from Chicago on their way to California had been relegated to secondary duties with the coming of the diesel; the *Orange Blossom Special* and the other deluxe trains from New York to Florida had put their steam engines aside in favor of electrics as far as Washington and diesels beyond that point. Some railways, however, had been slower to respond to the new temptations: the Norfolk & Western, which disdained the notion of store-bought locomotives and constructed its own proud beauties, held out for years; and the New York Central, whose squadrons of Hudsons and Mohawks set forth daily under the stewardship of P. W. Kiefer (Chief Engineer, Motive Power and Rolling Stock) was still faithful to steam. True, the latter railroad was experimenting with diesel switchers—the Great

Steel Fleet, as the Central fondly named its choice assortment of fast, long-distance passenger trains, was working out of Albany and up the West Albany hill with two or three of these diesels boosting them from the tail end—but the line's new high-speed special, the *James Whitcomb Riley*, running between Chicago and Cincinnati, was being hauled by a streamlined steam locomotive, and so was its equally famous *Empire State Express*.

The engineers who guided the steam locomotives in the early 1940s disliked the diesels, but later, as these men were mustered out of service, they were succeeded by men who expressed no overwhelming enthusiasm for the dust, the dirt, the smoke—the rattle, bang, and thump—of the steam engine. In the railroad YMCA just north of Union Station in Albany, engine crews who had been shifted from the 0-8-0 steam switchers to the new diesel yard locomotives were thundering that they hoped the damned new machines would fall apart. Some of these dissidents must have guessed that the diesel would introduce a whole new life-style on the railways, a style that would require a far smaller contingent of engineers and firemen and hostlers and shopmen. They were, of course, correct. Others felt that their own skills as psychiatrists and diagnosticians, their ability to discern the variations in temperament and whims among all the steam locomotives of a certain class—variations that were implicit in the fact that these engines were all in essence handmade—would be without value when they took over the helms of mass-produced machines that lacked in character what they made up for in efficiency. They, too, were correct.

Among those who would also miss the steam engine were the cameramen assigned by the War Department to record for the Office of War Information what they saw as they explored the roundhouses and yards. Their handiwork, many samples of which are seen in these pages, proclaims the pleasure that Charles Clegg and Richard Kindig and the rest of those wholly committed photographers of the steam engine found in their work. (Most of these pictures are making their first public appearance here.)

When the United States entered the Second World War, most railways were in transition from steam to diesel. Many managements had already opted for a full-scale conversion to diesels, while others moved cautiously; some chief mechanical engineers were putting diesels to work in yards and along industrial sidings, others were assigning them to long-haul freight runs, still others were cautiously thinking of completely replacing steam power on one division and giving the diesel a chance to prove itself as a man-of-all-work.

But for the most part, the "divisional points" on the railways remained during the war what they had been ever since railroads began—hostelries of, by, and for the steam locomotive. Before the days of interdivisional runs, the major divisional points were where the power on every train—passenger or freight, local or express—was taken off the head end and given a thorough "rubdown" before its next turn of duty. Such major points were as elaborate and extensive as the racing stables of a millionaire cotton or oil magnate, and they were as well staffed as a resort hotel that must be in service twenty-four hours a day on behalf of its exacting clientele; even before the war trains were rolling through divisional points at any time of day or night. Many of the towns around them would never have come into existence if these divisional points had not been set up, and the

rise and fall of these communities paralleled exactly the rise and fall of the steam engine. Modern engines, which no longer needed a rubdown every 150 miles, did not even halt in these little towns for servicing, and some of them have disappeared from the map.

The grandest divisional point of them all was surely the Norfolk & Western's setup at Roanoke, Virginia, where this railway's homemade steam engines were not only born but were maintained in the best of health for all of their long lives. The magnificent care bestowed by a staff who had looked after these locomotives since their birth and who understood every quirk and foible of each engine's individual personality is the reason that this fleet endured to become the last of its kind to compete with the diesel on any major American railway. Circumstance made the Norfolk & Western a well-heeled patrician, and it spent its money where it should have been spent. Had there been more railroads of its kind, the diesel might even today have been only an upstart, not the ruler. With its stately steam locomotives, the N&W served the shipping public, the traveling public, and even the railway buff, in a fashion truly grand.

Roanoke, with its erecting shop, its machine shops, its coaling and watering and greasing and repairing facilities, was a model by which all other divisional points could be judged. But more casual divisional points also come to mind—enterprises more characteristic of the American genus. The city of Roanoke could surely carry on even if it were no longer a divisional point, but those in the 1940s who saw the little town of Belleville, in northern Kansas—where an eastbound line of the Rock Island forked into two long extensions (to Omaha, to Kansas City)—must have wondered how it could manage without the railway. . . .

In Belleville, during the war, the Rock Island setup is rather like an open-air carnival—nothing at all resembling the elaborate Roanoke complex. On a summer midafternoon, up to a dozen steam engines are scattered about, some simmering in various degrees after the day's work, others getting up steam for the night ahead. A hostler or two is administering to the machines that are being readied to go out. Five or six men who have just brought in a freight train from the west are walking south across the yard trackage to where they left their automobiles, one, two, three days ago. They are wearing overalls or coveralls, bandanna sort of scarfs at the neck, and cloth caps; two of them, when they lift the heavy, rubber-framed goggles from their eyes, look like owls—their eyes stare out of skin-white ovals that are almost engulfed by a surround of coal-black dirt. All are carrying big tin lunch boxes and a thermos bottle or two. As the weary arrivals cross the tracks, a yard crew is climbing aboard the engine that has brought the freight into town; this crew will move it to a siding where a hostler can look it over. Another engine is being coupled on to the rear end of the freight, which will soon become one, two, maybe three other trains—a hotshot for Omaha, a hotshot for Kansas City, a peddler doing local work along one of these routes.

The yard crews, the hostlers, whatever machinists are on hand live in Belleville; the crews of the freight trains don't really live anywhere. Some of the latter have houses and wives in Belleville—wives who see them only three or four days a week, who launder what they can of the incredibly soiled clothes, who fill thermos bottles and lunch pails when their men go on the road again, who make sure as they send them off that their husbands' overalls or coveralls are tucked into their high, ungainly boots (a loose trouser leg can catch on something and drag a man to his death). Away from home, the men sleep in cubicles in a railroad YMCA with a shower bath at the end of the hall; when their lunch buckets have been emptied, they live on YMCA fried potatoes and gray roast beef and ketchup and coffee when they get up or before they go to bed. Sometimes they go to bed at seven-thirty in the morning; sometimes they get up at two in the morning. If they are on a peddler run, they most likely spend the night in their caboose, sleeping in their work clothes and cooking food that is no closer to a balanced diet than their dinners at the YMCA. Mealtime talk runs a steady pattern:

"Haven't seen Sam Godwin in a long time."

"Well, when his train went on the ground just west of Mankato, the stove in his caboose broke loose and pinned him against the head bulkhead."

"Pete Wallace bid in Sam's job."

"Pete says he thinks his boy is in Africa now, but he can't tell from the letters he gets from him."

"Well, good night."

If these men can be spared for a moment in wartime, they take time off for a holiday. There are two sorts of holidays. If it's summer, they fish. All these men have been around the railroad long enough to have passes that can be used over the whole Rock Island system. If they don't have an automobile, or if they don't have enough gasoline, they can travel, bit by bit, on the Rock Island's passenger and freight trains until they reach the handsome, rolling corn country in Iowa where bodies of water that bear names like Spirit Lake lie. If they can get there by passenger train, they can take their wives; wives, too, can travel on passes. The men fish. Fishing is calm, unhurried, sedentary.

If the holiday is a winter one, the men move south. They are lucky: Traffic Control has been going on the radio to ask everyone who doesn't have to travel to stay home, but holidays for people who have been working the way these men have are considered legitimate. So they board maid-of-all-work trains, made up almost entirely of mail, baggage, and express cars, that no one in his right mind—except, perhaps, people who have spent a few winters in northern Kansas—would think of riding the full distance to warm country. Two weeks in better weather, and the Belleville railroad men are then back in their overalls and coveralls and their YMCA cubicles.

The contrasts in the styles of life enjoyed, or put up with, by the traveling railway men were immense. Even today, in New York City's uninvitingly reconstructed Pennsylvania Station, there lurks along the lower level, where no civilian would suspect its existence, a full-fledged railway YMCA underground, with beds and showers and meals and a television-and-card room, just as it existed during the Second World War. (It should be noted that until well after the First World War traveling employees of the New York Central had a red-brick YMCA on the east side of New York's Park Avenue, where a far less picturesque topless tower now stands.) And a hundred or so miles north of New York City is the rather less prominent town of Maybrook, which in the 1940s consisted of no more than a big brick railroad YMCA beside an interchange yard in the midst of a woodland. The YMCA sat there because freight trains of the Erie, the Lehigh & Hudson River, and the New York, New Haven & Hartford met day after day to exchange courtesies and cars. An occasional wayfarer from the New York, Ontario & Western also would turn up, with more freight cars in hand. Like the yard it served, this YMCA was an all-day, all-night operation.

Not all the freight trains began or ended their runs in places like Roanoke or Belleville or even Maybrook. Many of them began at stations of such insignificance that the men who worked them had no place at all to lodge themselves conveniently. More than halfway across Iowa, on the Burlington line from Chicago to Omaha, there nestles, just north of the main line, the hamlet of Villisca. Winter and summer, during the forties, an engine or two sat beside this line, awaiting the arrival of the night mail-and-express job from Chicago. These were not engines for connecting express trains; they were the motive power for the mixed trains that worked southwest along the two branches that ended up by joining the Burlington's main line between Omaha and Kansas City. They were slow but useful beasts of burden—carrying parcels, letters, farm machinery, fertilizer, milk cans, newly hatched chicks in cardboard containers, a scattering of civilians, a few soldiers or sailors in undress uniform and on furlough, sometimes a brace of military in parade uniform escorting a casket draped in an American flag.

The men who worked these trains lived trackside at Villisca in a bunkhouse like hundreds of other bunkhouses that dotted the railway network in those days—bunkhouses under the command of the hundreds of motherly, middle-aged Mrs. McClarens and Mrs. Gilhooleys, who seemed to have been put upon earth solely to minister to the needs of men like those who worked the mixeds from Villisca out and back. Plain home cooking, a dozen little bedrooms, a copy of *Labor* and the most recent bulletin from the Brotherhood of Locomotive Engineers on the table in the hall, lights out at 10:00 P.M., if you please. A modicum of comfort and a vast convenience were the principal attributes of these many homes-away-from-home; picturesqueness was not included. Except, of course, in the case of Lone Pine, an outpost of the Southern Pacific in the bleak grandeur of the Owens Valley, northwest of Los Angeles, out where narrow-gauge country began. The McClaren/Gilhooley cuisine there was a cut above the rest, and the stunning mountainscape spread before the front veranda could not have greatly changed since the time of the forty-niners.

In his time, Ernest Hemingway wrote something about "men without women," though the characters he had in mind were quite unlike the crews of the Rock Island and the Burlington and the Lehigh & Hudson River and the Southern Pacific. "Men *away from* women" might be a better appellation for these railway men. Wartime or peacetime, their paths of communication with the outsider, the "civilian," the nonrail person, have always been narrow and devious. Like the Basque shepherds whom the Union Pacific and the ranchers of Nevada imported from northern Spain with special U.S. government permission to load the cattle cars out in the Big Sky country, railway men had then, and have now, little to say to outlanders: the language is not the same, the meanings and implications of commonplace words are not the same, the life experience has but minute points of contact. . . .

Belleville, and its myriad counterparts: there is a war overseas—and a war here, too, fought against snow that is riding almost horizontal on the wind. Mittens and mufflers are not quite enough to withstand such an assault, nor can the heating devices—when, indeed, there are any in the early forties—keep the innumerable switches in the yard warm enough to melt the snow. The track that stretches east and west is single, but it is so well signaled that the Interstate Commerce Commission, whose word is law in these matters, usually allows passenger trains to run along it at seventy-nine miles an hour. We are on a westbound express for Belleville on a zero-temperature day, traveling much slower than that: a westbound train is ahead of us, a troop train with valuable military equipment, and for that reason the War Department does not want it to run faster than forty miles an hour. But more than half the passengers on our train are also involved, one way or another, in the making of war, and their time is valuable, too; the divisional dispatcher would like to order the troop train to head in at the next siding so that he can run the express around it.

But the troop train has now come to halt a hundred feet east of a signal whose aspect is an uncompromising red, and the rear-end brakeman has climbed down from a tourist Pullman and—taking his lantern, his torpedoes, his fuses, and his life in his hands—is walking back east. He knows that the express is "on his time"—meaning it is due at that moment—and he must give warning.

The signal is red because a rail has snapped in the intense cold. From the divisional bunkhouse a group of men emerge, mount a speeder with the maintenance tools they know will be needed, and disappear eastward into the blizzard toward the broken rail. Meanwhile, the hostlers in the yard are making ready an extra engine to go west; it has been decided that, since the thermometer is falling a steady two degrees an hour, more than one locomotive will be needed to keep up the steam heat in the troop train that night. A pair of switch engines has put together a long freight booked to go east the minute the westbound express and the troop train have cleared. The broken rail is soon replaced. By morning it is as if nothing at all had gone wrong.

It was not simply the tonnage and the weather and accidents like that broken rail that all but over-whelmed the manpower on the rails, in the round-houses, and at the divisional points. Inexperienced and inadequate personnel were also a problem. The manpower authorities who determined which industries were more essential than others seemed at first not to understand that not everyone could be trusted to help run a railway system that was operating, al-legedly, at capacity or better. Men between ages eighteen and forty-five were being conscripted by the armed forces, and for a time the railways had to re-cruit whoever was available and willing—despite the consequences. For example: A man who had retired years before from the Southern Pacific was rehired during the war, at the age of seventy-seven. One evening after a local train had gone onto a siding at his station to let the *Argonaut,* an express from Chicago to the West Coast, go through, he suddenly decided that the switch that led off the main line had not been properly lined up. Throwing the switch an instant before the *Argonaut* arrived, he accidentally sent the express onto the siding and into the local train.

On another occasion, a new hand on the Pennsyl-vania noticed—en route—that there was a defective knuckle in the coupling that attached the rearmost Pullman sleeping car to a westbound express; instead of stopping the train, he dropped a length of thin wire into the knuckle. By some magic, this improvi-sation held things together until, part way up Horse Shoe Curve, west of Altoona, the knuckle gave way and the Pullman began to roll back down the steep, twisting incline. The porter on the car got his pas-sengers out of bed and moved them to the safer end of the car before it flew off the tracks. By doing this he saved most of them from injury, but he was killed in the derailment.

The realization that a little knowledge is a dangerous thing dawned upon Washington as a re-sult of such incidents, and matters were improved. Experienced men, sometimes brought out of retire-ment with the consent of the unions, taught the newcomers their crafts. Occasionally, a union man of one grade even threw a switch or opened a valve that by jurisdictional agreement should have been handled by a union man of another grade. And since all's fair in war as well as in love, the union "sea lawyers" who complained whenever that kind of thing happened were told by their comrades to lay off.

Working with the military brought peculiar prob-lems. Now and then, on the theory that all railways should have a go at moving troop trains, a main move was routed over a freight line whose divisional points no longer had—or never had had—facilities for putting aboard drinking water and water for the sanitary facilities and the kitchen cars. Often shop-men, summoned to repair a few malfunctioning de-vices on military trains, came upon machinery of a type they had never even seen before, much less worked on.

And then there was the military mind. One main move was routed from Chicago to Kansas City on a line so circuitous that the train commander, awaking at midnight, insisted that he could see the northern lights flickering over Hudson Bay; awaking again at dawn, he was shocked to discover himself and his train indeed pointing toward the Arctic Circle—and situated 175 miles away from Kansas City, where his caravan was due at that moment. The line thereto pointed south; he had been ordered (for some occult military reason) to bring the train into Kansas City in the order in which it had departed from Chicago, but now it had to be towed, stern first, to its destination, and it arrived six hours late. Soon after, military mind and civilian mind got together once more in the Pentagon, and all was adjusted. Trial and error, of course—over and over again—but it worked: we won the war, didn't we?

On a cold, windy, snowy night, the large, well-lit roundhouse is a hubbub of activity. Even from afar, great noises can be heard emanating from this lair of giants. The time could be 11:00 P.M., it could be 12:30 A.M., or 3:40, or 5:00, for that matter—almost anytime—for railroading is a seven-days-a-week, round-the-clock business. Across the bleak field and beyond the parking lot, the tools of the army of machinists, pipe fitters, boilermakers, and blacksmiths can be heard over the steamy din. This is a busy place, and the great increase of traffic on the railroad has made it necessary to go on a full shift, round the clock.

Opposite, inside the house, the call boy (above left) is busy on the phone calling crews and posting their names on the big assignment board. The cylinder to the left of the clerk is the pool board, listing the names of the men and the order, assignment, and trick (shift) they'll work. Crews register in at the clerk's office (above right); the conductor (below left) signs a separate sheet and picks up waybills and orders. Overalls are donned, and timepieces are checked with the official clock. Every man in a crew will go by the same official time—right to the second! If time permits, the local beanery is a sure bet. (DELANO)

As of January 1, 1939, 18.6 percent of all the railroads' steam locomotives were unserviceable. By December 7, 1941, the percentage of unserviceable locomotives had been reduced to 9.2. Then, because of the shortage of metal, allocations of steel and other materials necessary for the construction of new locomotives were reduced, and the railroads were told to *really* tighten their belts! *Make do with what's on hand!* became a war cry on the home front, and the shop forces went to work.

On these pages, the first trick is going to work (opposite) and foremen study their work schedules (right). Below, right, a boilermaker and his helper, from the shift going off, look over the work orders for the men who will start where these men left off. (DELANO)

Before starting work, the men listen to the daily report from the safety committee. The newer men are reminded: "Don't wear clothes that hang loose—especially shirts that don't stay tucked in to your coveralls—and always walk, *never run!*" Everyone is reminded to pay attention to what he is doing. "In every phase of your work on the railroad, each action, whether it's performed by one of you on foot, or by a member of a train crew with a mile-long train, must be made with care in order to avoid accidents. *Think!* Don't help Hitler by wearing a bandage on your finger!"

Below, a locomotive in off the run receives light (or *running*) repairs in the stall of the roundhouse. After every run, a locomotive inspector "writes up an engine" after examining it and going over the comments entered on a form by the engineer when the crew registers in. A hostler immediately cleans (or *drops*) the fire, and moves the engine into the house, over an inspection pit. Other inspectors go over the locomotive checking for steam leaks and worn parts. The roundhouse foreman will be given a written checklist report on the spot, and men will be put on the job to make the necessary repairs.

The last chore is the lubrication, using lubrication guns that work off of house air or the locomotive's own steam. Every thirty days, boilers are washed out, gauges and water glasses are cleaned, and all rigid stay bolts are hammer-tested to determine which are cracked or broken. (DELANO, WOLFER COLLECTION, DELANO)

On the following pages, men and women work on locomotives receiving their Four-Year Inspection. During that inspection all flues are removed from the boiler and the interiors are scaled and cleaned so that braces, riveted joints, and seams may be examined. Flues that can be reused are trimmed and "safe-end" welded. (left page, above left and below left, WOLFER COLLECTION; others, DELANO)

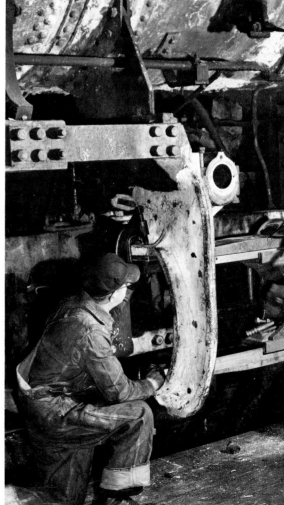

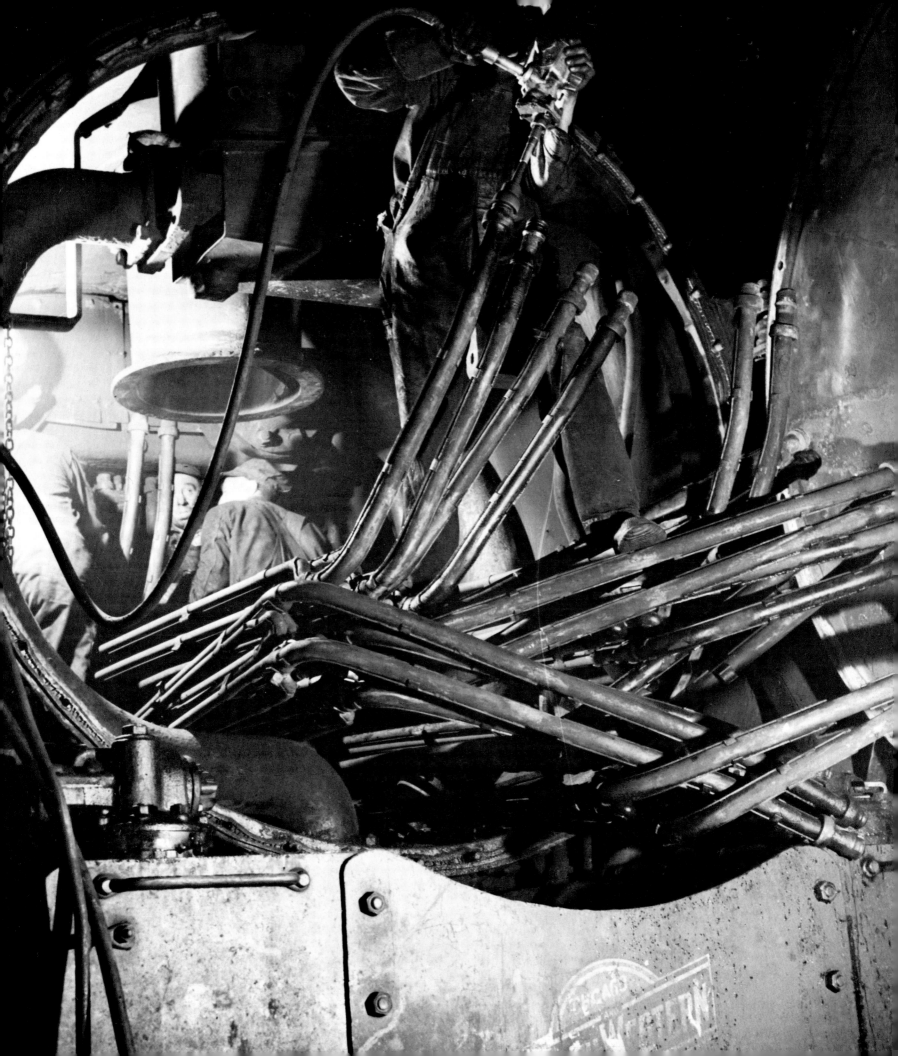

Under federal law, all steam locomotives must have each of the following: Monthly Inspection, Quarterly Test, Annual Inspection, Two-Year Examination of Stay Bolts, Four-Year Inspection, and Five-Year Examination.

"If it's got a good boiler, firebox, and cylinders, use it!" On this page, a former switch engine is shown being rebuilt into a road engine as part of the railroads' intensive effort to use every available piece of equipment in its potentially most useful role. Opposite, a locomotive receives its Five-Year Examination. Every five years, all of the jacket and lagging must be entirely removed and the exterior of the boiler gone over—completely—to determine its condition. A hydrostatic test is then administered to determine if there are any cracks or other failures that would "blow" under steam pressure.

On all railroads, each class of engines develops problems peculiar to its type and shop forces soon become accustomed to such idiosyncrasies. Some engines require two boiler washouts per month, others require new back flue sheets every two years, or whatever. In every case, shopping schedules are set up to try to match the needs—and peculiarities—of every given class. (DELANO)

A locomotive's Quarterly basically requires the removal and testing of steam gauges, setting of safety valves, and orifice tests on the air compressors. On this spread (clockwise from above), class 3, 4 and 5 repairs are in process on the Illinois Central, Santa Fe, and Central Vermont.

Across the land, on every railroad, the story is the same: men and women working around the clock, keeping the locomotives' time spent in the shops at a minimum.

Standard practice is for the railroad to locate its main shop at a "central" point, or to maintain several main shops at points along the system where freight traffic is heaviest and the greatest number of locomotives will be accessible for repairs. Such central points are usually not the geographical centers on the railroads but rather the business centers of each system. Many railroads create a small shop within the roundhouse, independent of the main shop, for light repairs. Such a shop usually includes both a machine shop and blacksmith shop. Other roads maintain an inventory of machine tools in a roundhouse to perform certain machining work that might tie up the larger shop. Opposite, under agreement with the unions, twenty minutes for lunch. (COLLECTION, HASTINGS, DELANO)

Each railroad has a locomotive shop (or *erecting shop* or *back shop*) to carry out the inspections required and to make all repairs. The shops are huge and are usually *longitudinal shops,* ones in which everything is arranged parallel with the general line of yard tracks. Standard practice is for locomotives to enter and leave the shop on two, three, or more central (or *working*) tracks. No turntable or transfer table is necessary, since locomotives are carried overhead to the working space (or *bay*) by huge traveling cranes. Some railroads have a separate boiler shop, in addition to the erecting and machine shops. Locomotives entering the shop for all classes of repairs are stripped and then unwheeled in the boiler shop, where crane service is available. When necessary, boilers are removed from frames in the boiler shop, and the skeleton and machinery are then transferred to the erecting shop by a transfer table; wheels are usually handled by a traveling jib crane. Each part is given the locomotive or lot number, usually prefixed by R or $L,$ for right or left side.

Almost anything requiring repairs can happen to a working locomotive, but the things that usually do happen are the result of the natural wear and tear of regular service. All railroad locomotive shops have to be prepared to perform operations such as re-turning or re-tiring wheels; refitting boxes, side rods, pistons, and so on; replacing, say, boiler tubes or firebox sheets; and repairing a multitude of minor parts—everything usually on short notice! (DELANO)

The typical shop has separate departments, machines, and manpower to handle: locomotive cylinders; piston and piston rings; piston valves, cages, and rings; crossheads and guides; connecting rods; driving boxes; shoes and wedges; eccentrics and links; locomotive frames; driving wheels and axles; pipes and parts; air pumps and hoses; et cetera, et cetera. The blacksmith shop, pattern shop and boiler shop, and tank (or *tender*) shop are separate operations, usually in adjacent buildings.

Opposite, a huge locomotive is up on the blocks and ready for *wheeling*. The four pairs of driving wheels and their axles will be rolled into position under the locomotive and blocked in correct position on the track. The overhead crane with its two hooks will lower the great boiler by means of two slings, fore and aft, after the wood cradle is taken down. The driver boxes have been placed upon the axle journals, so that when the locomotive is lowered by the crane, the boxes will enter the corresponding jaw openings in the frame. Meanwhile, the rod gang makes the necessary repairs to the locomotive's main rods and side rods, together with all allied parts. All rods have been thoroughly cleaned and inspected for any fractures, the thickness of both front- and back-end bearings checked for wear, and brasses cleaned and examined. Above, a machinist grinds away rough edges left by the milling machine. (DELANO, WOLFER COLLECTION)

Strip a big, modern locomotive of its side motion and valve gear; remove the driving wheels and boxes from under the frame; open up the cylinders, steam chest, and boiler (*smokebox*) front; remove the cab from the end, and the jacket and its underlying lagging of asbestos from the entire length of the boiler. Then drop the naked boiler and its exposed frame upon 10-inch cribbing placed across the shop pit—and you have before you the skeleton of a huge machine that (under the efforts of a vast army of machinists, pipe fitters, boilermakers, metalworkers, and their helpers) will be overhauled, repaired, and refitted until it assumes once more its spectacular appearance, and, restored to its full working capacity, is ready again for service on the road. (COLLECTION, COLLECTION, WOLFER COLLECTION)

The railroad has never been a place for a woman! In 1941 there are over 750 name-trains in the United States—but only two of them are named after women. Trains are named for men, trees, birds, flowers, cities, and states—but not for women! Chief Powhatan's daughter, Pocahontas, and Abe Lincoln's first sweetheart, Ann Rutledge, have the honor for now. (After the war, there will be a *Kate Shelley 400* and the revival of *Phoebe Snow*.)

During the war and the *man*power shortage, few railroad departments remain uninvaded by women. In 1942, 320,000 railroad jobs needed immediate filling as the War Department continued skimming the cream of rail labor for its Military Railway Service. The Santa Fe, Southern, Pennsylvania, and New York Central were even training four engineer battalions out of their ranks for the Army. Clearly, women were the answer. Women gatemen and ushers showed up in big PRR stations, and women were also hired by Pennsy to clean engines and coaches; the Reading put women to work on the tracks; the Boston & Maine hired women for yard brakeman jobs, and so on. Women soon were riveting locomotives, announcing trains, working on the drafting boards. They are certainly visible in these scenes at the busy San Bernardino shops, servicing the locomotives of the Santa Fe and Union Pacific in 1943. (DELANO)

127

Teamwork and cooperation are vital in keeping the trains on the go. One failure by one person at one task can tie up a whole railroad—especially if the failure is out on the road. While crews are reporting in for work, fire builders, engine watchmen, and hostlers are readying the locomotives, making sure everything is ready to go at the called-for time. Delays at the roundhouse could force the engine dispatcher to substitute a locomotive at the last minute—which might mean a dissatisfied engine crew at the start of the run, additional work for the fireman during the run, and, finally, a delay in the schedule at the end of the run. THIS MUST NOT HAPPEN!

In almost assembly-line fashion, the hostlers move the great locomotives under the huge coaling dock for coal and sand; one by one, engines are spotted under the chutes, filled and topped off, and, after taking on water, moved out to the ready tracks. Fires are continually checked and cleaned. It is important to turn the engine over to the road crew with a well-coked fire with the steam pressure within fifty pounds of the maximum boiler capacity. Incidentally, depending on whether the fire is red-hot or white-hot, the temperature inside that M-4's firebox is between 2,000 and 3,000 degrees! With a working pressure of, say, 200 pounds, the pressure on the firebox sheets is over 3,000 tons! Everyone must be conscientious on the job. (DELANO, BALL, DELANO)

After the pumps are thawed and the train's air pumped up, the locomotive opposite will depart, pulling one of the fifteen new freight trains that start out on their runs *every minute,* day and night, across the land! The railroads are moving over two million freight cars—constantly—marshaling them where they're needed, keeping battlefield supplies moving. *Each minute,* some 1.3 million tons of freight will travel a distance of one mile! Back in the roundhouse is a sign no one forgets: SAVING MINUTES HERE SAVES LIVES ON THE BATTLEFIELD.

At right, the engineer—*hogger* to the railroader—relaxes for a moment while his fireman examines the ashpan to see that it has been properly cleaned out and no green coal remains that might ignite. He will also check the tender's coal pile, check the stoker, and make sure the proper flagging equipment and all necessary road tools are provided. Below, the fire has been built up with a scoop in anticipation of the initial hard work and correspondingly heavy steam requirements when they start to pull. The engineer is always responsible for the locomotive and its performance on the road; the fireman is responsible to the engineer. (DELANO, DELANO, BALL)

January 1943, and at Casablanca the Allied leaders are reaffirming their intention to beat Hitler first, despite the pressure on the American home front to concentrate on Japan. At Rabat, President Roosevelt pays a surprise visit to our troops in Africa. No President has ever left the United States in wartime, and it is the first time in eighty years—since Lincoln went to Gettysburg—that a President has visited a battle theater. On the home front, by the end of January, it is already quite evident the railroads are going to easily surpass their impressive records of 1942. The huge American industrial machine has been fully harnessed for war.

The next several pages are spent "on location" in the yard; the man in charge is pictured opposite. He's the yardmaster, and he is overall boss; he's in charge of the whole yard, its employees, and the movement of trains and engines within the yard limits. Distribution of the cars within the yard also comes under his jurisdiction. He reports to, and receives his instructions from, the trainmaster.

At right, and below, the assistant yardmaster confers with a switchman and yard helper about special work orders accompanying military supplies on a cut of cars being "kicked" by the switch engine. (DELANO)

Opposite, a young fireman and his engineer climb into their engine, preparing to couple on to their train. The head brakeman will soon join them. The conductor will also come on board with duplicate train orders and go over them with the train crew. After coupling, and pumping up the air, the slack will be stretched to make sure that all couplings are secure. On signal, the engineer will move the brake valve into service application, and yard inspectors will walk the length of the train to inspect the brakes. Car inspectors (at right and below) carefully check each journal for proper lubrication and to see that cars carrying gasoline and explosives are so marked, with all required instructions and regulations clearly indicated. Obviously, strangers or persons not on railroad business are unwelcome; sabotage in a rail yard is a distinct possibility, and many rail yards have armed personnel. The engineer makes certain that the air brakes permit complete train control, and as soon as he receives brake clearance from the assistant yardmaster, he will "whistle off" and another freight train will be on its way. (DELANO)

The dawn of a new day: a bright sunny morning, a new first trick—and the trains arriving and departing, under the watchful eyes of the inspectors.

Opposite, a switchman waits for the arriving train he is to work. Above, teamwork between brakeman, fireman, and engineer. By day, the trainmen and yardmen use arm and hand signals to indicate to engine crews almost everything: coupling distance; forward, backward; commands to get into the clear, pull out, shove, take water—or break for lunch! By night, the hand lantern, with its tongue of fire, speaks the same language.

On this page, car inspectors walk the line carefully looking over a train that has stopped for a change of power. Inspectors always work under flag protection; a blue flag is placed on each end of the train as notice that the train cannot be moved. When the work is completed and the train ready to roll, the blue flags are removed—*but only by the inspector who placed them there.* (DELANO)

To the average layman, railroad yards are a confusing maze of tracks, but not to the railroad man. Switching lists are always prepared in advance of a train's arrival, and when it pulls in, work is immediately started—breaking up and reassembling the train, blocking the cars in new trains for their various destinations. The yardmaster, switch foreman, and the crews, working with one another, break down arriving trains and reclassify the cars into new trains as efficiently as possible, for any one failure will result in a nightmare of congestion. Those cars opposite with the white X are carrying explosives. They are cut off the inbound train and are being protected at the rear until they can be classified into their new train. (DELANO)

While prompt handling of loads in transit is greatly desired, the prompt disposition and efficient use of empties is just as important, for each car is a weapon of war, loaded or empty. Many other details must be looked after in the yard, such as the return of foreign line cars, reicing of refrigerator cars in transit, feeding and watering of livestock, quick repairs of equipment. Here, while a cut of sixty empty stock cars clumps by, the men take a breather. (DELANO)

Down at the "business end of the yard," as soon as a freight train is made up and inspected, the road engine and caboose are coupled on. Every conductor and engineer has received duplicate train orders. Watches are compared and set. The train's air is pumped up. Opposite, the head brakeman gives his train the highball and the engineer opens the throttle. Several tracks over, another locomotive, bell ringing, starts out of the yard with its train.

At right, above, another inbound freight arrives, its engine puffing tumbling smoke into the cold winter air, keeping a mile of train and stiff journals on the move. Below, a switchman walks ahead "bending the iron"—putting the train on its assigned track. Within minutes, the "yard goats" will move in and grab cuts of cars, quickly reclassifying them into sequences (or *blocks*) according to points of destination. New trains will continue on. In the yard office, clerks checking the switch list look over every train's consist—car by car—and make up cards that are tacked on to those cars that are to be cut out of an arriving train. (DELANO)

On the following pages: a look at the beauty in winter steam-railroading. (DELANO)

No portrait of a railroad yard is complete without a look at a gravity hump, tower, electro-pneumatic retarders, and hump engine. An inbound train is shoved over the hump; working in the tower from a switch list, the humpmaster controls the yard's switches, setting them for each car that rolls down the hump. At the base of the tower, on the crest, a pin-puller, working with a duplicate switch list, uncouples the cars as they roll slowly by. He and the man in the tower communicate with each other by speaker-phone so that cars won't end up on the wrong track. As each car gathers speed, it rolls through the retarder (above), where retarder beams bob up under air pressure, spring-clamping the car's wheels to slow its momentum. With a squeal and a shuddering bang the car almost stops, then rolls slowly the rest of the way down its right track and into its train. At right—last, but certainly not least—the caboose rolls by gravity down to its train as the brakeman controls its coupling speed by setting the hand brake. Opposite, the conductor's highball. (DELANO)

3

OUT
ON
THE
LINE

Pine Bluff, Arkansas, 5:00 P.M.: The man in the divisional offices of the Cotton Belt has been at or near his desk since quarter to six that morning. He is waiting for the *Cotton Belter,* a passenger train that went north out of Dallas at eight o'clock carrying a friend of his from the New York Central. Both men will soon be called to Washington to sit at desks in Traffic Control's headquarters in the Pentagon, but neither knows this yet. The New York Central man has recently moved from his post as assistant division superintendent at Albany, through which the Central runs a four-track main line. Now a "roving expediter," he has been down in Dallas at the request of someone in the Office of Defense Transportation who would like a few suggestions for expediting the movement of tonnage and troops through the complicated skein of tracks that enmesh Dallas Union Station. The Cotton Belt man is a division superintendent. His main line is single track.

The train from Dallas pulls into Pine Bluff; the man from the Central alights, and a yard switcher pops the nightly Saint Louis sleeper on to the rear end. It is a first-rate sleeper, and because it is open

season on ducks, it would ordinarily be filled with hunters going home to Saint Louis: the country north from here to Stuttgart and Paragould is made for duck hunters. But in wartime, the passengers the train picks up this afternoon and evening at Pine Bluff have more important matters on their minds. So has the Central man, who is on the prowl around the United States to see how other railroads are handling wartime problems. Tonight he ponders a task that seems clearly impossible; his friend shows him the Pine Bluff chart: yesterday's trains—23 northbound freights, 23 southbound freights, 2 passenger trains each way, 3 troop trains each way—all over a single track.

"I can't believe you can get that much tonnage over the road like that," says the visitor.

The single-track Cotton Belt man smiles at his four-track New York Central colleague—a slow, friendly, Arkansas countryman smile. "You'll see how tomorrow," he promises.

The Cotton Belt, which is what everyone in the railroad business calls the Saint Louis Southwestern, was built to do that kind of job, and so was its motive power. Even after the heavy-duty war work was done and the diesels were pushing the steam locomotives aside, the Cotton Belt's steam engines were in such excellent health that the Southern Pacific, the foster father of the Cotton Belt, moved them to the West Coast to finish out their time. Career commuters in and out of San Francisco insist that these Cotton Belters were assigned regular turns on the commuter runs down to San Jose.

The Cotton Belt line itself extended no farther west than eastern Texas, and no farther east than the banks of the Mississippi, but it was an important link for the Southern Pacific, for it enabled that line to run its trains into the major railway center at Saint Louis. The eastern end of the Cotton Belt was—and still is—the town of Thebes, Illinois, well southeast of Saint Louis, but by acquiring running rights over a long stretch of Missouri Pacific, the Cotton Belt could run its trains not only to Saint Louis but to East Saint Louis, and its freight trains could thus bypass the vast and overloaded tangle of the Terminal Railroad Association of Saint Louis's trackage. The Cotton Belt was already running a posse of celebrated time freights—*The Blue Streak, The Motor Special, The Southwester, The Pacific Coaster*—from the Saint Louis Gateway to San Francisco, and by a variety of routes. Adding the steady procession of tank cars from Texas and the steady flow of troop trains to Texas was not really a problem for men like the division superintendent at Pine Bluff. . . .

The two men are on the road themselves the next day, going south by troop train. Officially, they are in the tourist sleeper drawing room that serves as office for the train commander; actually, they are leaning out of the Dutch door in a vestibule, so that the Cotton Belt man can point out the sights. On every siding they pass, a northbound tank train is lined up, but it is not stationary: it is moving slowly, so that the moment the troop train has cleared and the man waiting at the northern end of the siding has thrown the switch, the tank train will come out onto the main—a nonstop meeting, and a maneuver that is to be repeated all day long.

"We haven't had much train trouble," the New York Central man is saying. "What we have been having is brain trouble. We were hanging every ton of freight we could behind every Mohawk working west out of Selkirk Yard, south of Albany, in the order we wanted the cars to be in when they got where we wanted them to go. Then we discovered that even by the time the train got to Buffalo the cars had been rearranged, or sometimes had even been put on other trains. Somebody in the divisional office at Syracuse had been cutting the trains apart when they reached De Witt Yard, a few miles east of Syracuse, because he said they were too long to get over the road. There *is* a little grade against them just east of Batavia, but not enough to sink them. We've got that straightened out now."

"Yeah, well," responds the Cotton Belt man, "a friend of mine on the Santa Fe told me they were having the same trouble out in Arizona. With all the war traffic, the Santa Fe freights were getting to be longer than the Arizona state law allowed, and the trains were being cut in two at the state border—the Santa Fe was running out of train and engine crews. Somebody in the ODT had to get on the phone to the governor of Arizona and ask him to fix that up until the war's over."

Washington, D.C., January 4, 1942: The trainmaster in charge of operations in the capital has Traffic Control in the Pentagon on the phone. "I want a couple of you guys to come up here right away and look at something." A set of tourist sleepers has come into Washington Terminal on an overnight run from Boston—a full load of recruits, none of them yet in uniform. Every window in the train is cracked or punched out. Some of the corridor doors are off their hinges. Most of the wash basins and toilet bowls in the lavatories are smashed in, and some of the plumbing has been disconnected. "I wonder where those kids think the war is," the trainmaster asks Traffic Control. "Now what are you going to use for that 2:00 P.M. main move to Norfolk?"

While Traffic Control ponders these questions, the second section of Pennsylvania #111, *The Legislator,* out of New York that morning, arrives. It is 11:36 A.M.; First #111, with its parlor cars and its diner, came in on time, at 11:25. The second section now pulling in is made up entirely of P-70 coaches—the durable heavyweights that began their long careers in the early years of the century.

"There's nothing in the yards for that Norfolk move," the trainmaster says. . . . Then it hits him: "I wonder if the Pennsy knows where I'm going to send these P-70's of theirs?"

Peoria to Keokuk, July 1942: If the Chicago Fire had destroyed that city so thoroughly that it had had to be wholly rebuilt, most of its stations and freight yards, and most of the tracks that lead to them, would surely have been relocated to form a less complicated network; the Elgin, Joliet & Eastern, and the Toledo, Peoria & Western—railways that loop south of the solar plexus of the great Chicago complex to get around the congenital delays and congestion that are bad in peacetime and worse in wartime—would then not be needed.

The Toledo, Peoria & Western is only 224 miles long, but on that loop around Chicago it makes connections with other railways at no fewer than twenty-two junctions. Most laymen have never heard of it; everyone in the trade knows about it, and almost everyone uses it. It is not very well known to the public because it has no scheduled passenger service, and because its beginning point in the east is Effner, Illinois—and who ever heard of Effner?

Actually, the TP&W *does* carry passengers; the towns through which it passes are nearly all without bus services, and wartime rationing of gasoline has created such problems for motorists that travelers—most of them men—occasionally try the railway. But they take their chances, and their time: the through freights, which dust across the junction towns as determinedly as if they did not exist, must not be halted, for the needs of the military are too urgent. Instead, passengers must await the arrival of a local run—one of the freight trains that stop to set out and pick up cars at all of those twenty-two junctions; but not just any local will do—only one of them permits passengers. This local, moreover, runs only at night, and because it is always delayed to make way for the through runs, its published schedules come under the heading of light fiction. Few passengers ride this train, and when they do, they must ride the caboose. Such travelers are going, for the most part, to towns no more than thirty or forty miles away, and—as they board the caboose—they explain to the conductor that they are riding the freights because in wartime there is no other way. Passengers obviously are not a major commodity on the TP&W.

In wartime Peoria, passengers are considered with disfavor or with downright suspicion. Midtown seems to be made up entirely of crisscrossing railway lines, and all sorts of military goods are moving along them. A dozen tracks, side by side, lead past what is cheerfully termed Union Station, though only a few passenger trains stop there now. The TP&W yards, east of the town, seem endless—and they are in a sense, for the TP&W interchanges freight cars here with ten other railways. What lies inside many of those cars is the military's business only; the opportunities for a little sabotage at such a focal point as Peoria are plentiful.

In a hotel in downtown Peoria a man who has a War Department identification card in his pocket and a mission to be fulfilled—he says in Keokuk, across the Mississippi in Iowa—is making travel plans. There is a scheduled bus heading north on this thunder-and-lightning evening; the bus could take him to Chillicothe, a few miles up the Illinois River, where the Santa Fe would take him west over the Mississippi, and perhaps there is a morning bus south to Keokuk. Or he could take another roundabout route: north, west, and south—two changes of train en route, and long waits in between. But the TP&W is the route he wants. He telephones the TP&W yard office and is told that the railway does not carry passengers. He points out that the Official Guides rosters a westbound freight, due out of Peoria at 8:40 that night, that does carry passengers. "Who are you, anyway?" asks the man in the yard office, and the man in the hotel replies. The reply indicates that the journey is essential.

As the traveler finishes dinner a while later, two armed railway police come into the lobby, looking for him. In their car he is driven through the storm, which is now a continuous bombardment, to the yard office. It is 7:30. The stranger is put in a windowless cement-block room where two men are working at typewriters. No one speaks to him. He sits.

Finally, not long after midnight, the railway police return and, without a word, indicate that he is to follow them. Now a long journey through the yard, between freight trains and bits of freight trains that yard engines are switching about in the steady downpour; then a halt beside a caboose, and signals from the police indicating that he is to get aboard. They depart, still wordless. Wordless, too, are the men he discovers in the caboose. One of them indicates the bunk upon which the traveler is to sit. At

1:00 A.M., the train begins to move. It rolls slowly, without stopping, past Union Station—where unknowing passengers would (and with reason) expect it to stop, and moves on toward Keokuk.

The guest aboard local freight #123 this stormy morning actually has no mission in Keokuk. He is spending a sleepless night sitting bolt upright aboard the train because the Office of Defense Transportation, back in Washington, is wondering whether the recent disaffection between the management and the union men of the TP&W will bring about an interruption of service on this invaluable line. The guest is "looking around" to see "how things are." This is his first look. The subterfuge is necessary because a stranger who wants to travel a long way on a TP&W freight is clearly, to the employees of the railway, a company spy.

Freight #123 stops at towns with evocative names like Canton and Cuba to exchange carloads of this and that with the Burlington; it stops at a town with the workaday name of Bushnell to let an eastbound through freight hold the main line without stopping. When the men come back into the caboose after each of these stops, the rain that drips from their clothing starts tiny rivers wandering along the wooden floor. The conductor, working steadily at a sheaf of papers on his tiny desk, lights a cigar; its smoke, should it ever descend to floor level, would extinguish instantly the hardiest of cockroaches. At La Harpe (named by the French canotiers who came up the Mississippi two centuries ago?) there is a long pause, and one of the crew begins to brew coffee on the stove. The cup of jet-black fluid that he offers the guest is accompanied by the first words spoken to the traveler since he was deposited at the yard office in Peoria. The coffee cheers him; the spoken words relieve him: the crew has decided, in an offstage conference, that he is not a company spy. The conversation continues—and it is friendly—all the way into a magnificent dawn and Keokuk, at 6:45 A.M., six hours and fifteen minutes late. Keokuk is a riverboat town like those described by Mark Twain, and not noticeably altered in a hundred years, but the traveler has no time for enjoyment; he needs a few hours abed before his next "looking around."

What Washington worries about eventually happens: there *is* a violent disturbance on the TP&W, and later, George P. McNear, Jr., its president, is shot to death in his front yard. The ODT sends out its own man, John Barriger, to save the situation. But that is another story. . . .

Washington, D.C., to New York City, Friday, 4:00 P.M.: First Pennsylvania #152 is departing northbound from Washington Terminal—from the national capital the weekly homeward surge of wartime consultants, technicians, businessmen has begun. Though the trackage for a half-mile north is blanketed by a network of overhead catenary, the little bulldog steam switch engines are still moving on it everywhere. First #152, though—eleven heavyweight Pullman parlor cars, a Pennsy dining car, and one of that railroad's valiant GG1's, perhaps the finest electric locomotives ever built—will be hauled all the way to New York by the power that lies hidden in that catenary. She is the first section of the *Congressional Limited*—first stop Newark, New Jersey, in whatever time the engineer chooses to make it. On this day it is 189 minutes for the 214.8 miles. New York is 12 minutes and 10 miles farther—that includes the sharp dip under the Hudson River and the steep climb up into Pennsylvania Station. Two Pennsy men put away their watches. It is 7:21 when the train reaches New York, although the first section of the *Congressional* is not due until 7:35.

"Not bad," says one of the men.

"No," says the other, "but we made it at 7:19 three weeks ago."

Second #152—three parlors, a dining car, and a string of coaches—is out of Washington Terminal at 4:05. Her first stop is Thirtieth-Street Station, Philadelphia. She will pull in at New York at 7:33. At her stop in Newark, she picks up a fleet of unusual passengers—women aged anywhere from their thirties to their fifties, in overalls, shirts, wearing bandannas to bind their hair. As the train proceeds to New York, they move through the coaches, picking up, sweeping up the debris deposited by the hundreds of passengers. There will be no time to do this cleaning at Penn Station: the coaches will immediately become part of Second Pennsylvania #143, the *Mount Vernon,* due out of New York at 7:35—or as soon after that as six Pullman sleeping cars, all bound for points south of Washington on Southern Railway #29, can be drilled on to the south end of the string of coaches while a switch engine is removing the parlor cars from the north end.

Second #143 is away at 7:42, and as she begins to

move along one side of her platform, Third #152, from Washington, is pulling in on the opposite side of the platform—two Pullman parlors, a dining car, and more coaches. She has made all the stops en route that the tight-lipped timetable calls for (there is never a mention in that table of this Friday-night tripartite cavalcade of the northbound *Congressional Limited*).

Railroading has always been a men's club, by the way, but the women car cleaners who get aboard at Newark (and who sometimes have to shuttle back to New Jersey on the same evening before their "housekeeping" job is done) are not the only females in the gang now. There are women ticket sellers, women ticket collectors, women switch tenders, women turntable tenders, women working in yard offices. It is a breakthrough as big as the breaching of the German lines in the Battle of the Bulge.

Newton, Kansas, 3:00 A.M.: Santa Fe #23-27, the *Antelope,* has just moved off for Oklahoma City, six cars overweight and twenty minutes late—but it *has* departed. The second section, ten tourist Pullman sleeping cars, is on the platform, all its soldiers abed save for the train commander, a second lieutenant, who is talking to a pair of Sante Fe men. For all his short life the lieutenant has loved trains and railways; now he is having almost his fill of both. But not quite.

His train is waiting to see what the roundhouse will produce. Here comes the locomotive—one that for years has done work no more ennobling than hauling two- or three-car local trains or pulling a broken-down gas-electric rail car to its destination. The engine is a lightweight Atlantic—a 4-4-2—and tonight its assignment is to wheel a nine-hundred-ton train of tourist sleeping cars bound south for Ponca City, Oklahoma. The lieutenant does not attempt to hide his excitement. His perch all the way to Ponca City, three hours distant, is not the drawing room to which he is entitled but the vestibule at the head end of the first tourist Pullman. There he listens until daybreak to the sound of that Atlantic dealing—like so many people, so many other pieces of machinery—with a wartime task three times the size of the one for which its makers had designed it.

The highball has been given from the rear end and (opposite) the engineer whistles in the rear brakeman. Earlier, while backing the engine down to the train, the engineer opened up the back sanders for the last one hundred feet before coupling to insure a good coating of sand on the rail—a little trick veteran hoggers do for smooth starting.

From the right-hand seat box (right), the measured beats of exhaust are felt back in the cab—the feel of hundreds of tons of rolling steel giving a stiff, hard ride. The *womph-womph-womph-womph* sound from the stack gets louder as the throttle is widened. The head brakeman grabs the irons and swings aboard, and "we have the railroad." Cylinder cocks are opened momentarily. The engine rides rough—pounds—most likely from a loose or badly worn connecting rod cap. Sometimes high water in the boiler causes pounding. *Womph-womph-womph-womph* the orange-white glint of the fire dances behind the firebox doors at each exhaust; the fireman knows as long as his fire has enough hot coal evenly distributed, the heat it gives off is proportional to the draft, and the effect of the engine's exhaust makes it partly self-regulating. (DELANO, DELANO, HASTINGS)

Keep your mind on the railroad!—on the train and on your rear end (your caboose)! The throttle is closed, a slight air reduction made, and some slack runs in, giving us a kick in the tail. The whole train slows and we pick up a second conductor who will be riding the rear end, keeping an eye on the tanks and armored personnel carriers riding the flats. Opposite, the engineer works the injector and opens the throttle; at left, the fireman's mind is set on the amount of coal going in as he watches the color of the fire; occasionally he cracks the doors wide to look for banks and holes, which are always possible in a working engine. He knows that very seldom will any two engines have the same steaming qualities, so it's best to play it safe starting out on a run—by having a little extra water in the boiler to trade off for steam until you know the engine's steaming qualities and water pump capabilities. (YOUNG, BALL, NOWAK)

The struggle in wartime America comprises three great battles, whose outcomes—as history will prove—depend upon the mobile forces behind them. First, there is the battle on the fighting front itself, now spread to virtually all parts of the globe; second, there is the battle of production; and third, there's the battle of transportation. Safely moving the most tons the most miles in the quickest time is the railroad's offensive line. With a war train pounding along the railroad, everyone's duty out on the line is to *keep it moving!*

The chief dispatcher has charge of an entire division. Depending on the size of the railroad, he might have several assistants. He is responsible—*at all times!*—for knowing what trains are coming onto his division, as well as what is already operating over his division. Engine and train dispatchers give him power and crews as required. The train order is the dispatcher's means of running his part of the railroad, and operators along the line are responsible for copying instructions correctly, reading each one back to the dispatcher, and hooping 'em up to the conductor and engineer by a detachable string between the bamboo forks of an order hoop.

Above, as viewed from the cupola, the conductor "hooks the flimsies" from an operator along the line (duplicate orders were handed up to the head end). At left, at another location, the fireman snatches up orders, while the engineer keeps a keen eye on the track ahead. Opposite, the view from the caboose—the operator returning to his post, an order hoop in each hand. (DELANO, YOUNG, DELANO)

Another crew reports; another freight will soon be on the road. At right, up past the yard office locomotives steam by, shaking the snow-covered ground, parading by like trolley cars, en route to their assigned trains.

Enginemen work together as a team, but they are also alone; as each one works his assigned job on the locomotive, the dispatch and safety of thousands of tons of freight, or hundreds of passengers, hang on their vigilance and skill. They all experience the exhilaration of harnessing and directing great power, the feeling accentuated by the tremendous noise and motion of their machine. All their senses and faculties are called upon: their ability to see, to hear, to smell, to feel, to use their expertise and to think quickly and accurately at all times.

160

At right: the fireman's view from the left-hand cushion, down over the running board and along the great boiler of his locomotive. Below: a view across the jouncing deck, of the engineer widening out on the throttle, letting more and more steam do more and more work. Back on the left-hand side, every fireman dreams of the day he will be "set up" as engineer—when he'll cross the deck to the eminence of the right-hand cushion. Before the war and the manpower crunch, nearly every regular fireman was a qualified engineer, but the "true" engineers usually had thirty-five or more years of service behind them. Prewar, a fireman with fewer than fifteen years seniority was considered a man holding on to his job—and his scoop—by his eyebrows!

(DELANO, DELANO, DELANO, YOUNG)

On the rear end, in a world much quieter than the wheeled Hades on the head end, the alternating *click-click, clack-clack* picks up as the long train gathers speed. As the caboose leaves the yard, the conductor stands in the door-way, watching for any signals from yard personnel that might indicate something is wrong with the train. A wave from a trainman, towerman, switch engine crewman—any railroader—is not merely a friendly gesture, but a signal after the man has made a careful visual inspection of the train as it passes that "all's well." If anything is wrong, best to catch it right away, before something serious happens.

Bladank-bladank, bladank-bladank and we've rattled over the diamond at the end of the yard limit. Below: the brakeman's view of the yard from the swaying cupola—or *bird's nest*. Opposite: the view of the train from the back platform of the caboose. The brakeman takes advantage of every curve to check the train for telltale wisps of smoke or sparks, which could indicate that brakes have failed to release properly, or—worse yet—a hotbox. (DELANO)

The caboose, known also as a *crummy, hack, way car, buggy, cabin car,* and always, the *rear end,* is the train office and traveling home for the train crew. The freight conductor has his desk in the caboose, where he keeps the waybills, reports, and all other papers pertinent to the train. En route, he prepares a wheel report showing the origin, destination, and contents of each car in the train. Another typical activity en route could be the preparation of an ice list for refrigerator cars that are to be set out along the way; the conductor would then prepare the instructions, throw them off to an operator along the line who would wire the dispatcher, who in turn would wire the yardmaster or an operator up the line where the reefers are to be set out.

When an opposing train appears, the brakeman will get down from the cupola and get out on the rear platform to look over the passing train. Above, he signals "all's well" to his counterpart on the other train. At left: the decor of a railroader's home-away-from-home. Opposite: the rear office and the conductor. On the railroad, the freight conductor is known as "the skipper" or, more commonly, "the old man." (DELANO)

The caboose has lockers for clothing and supplies, a water cooler, icebox, tables, bunks, benches, nooks, crannies, and the good old iron stove with its ever-present coffeepot. Under each caboose is the toolbox (*possum belly,* to the railroader) with its rerailing frogs, blocking jacks, chains, tools, and other emergency equipment. Usually one member of the rear-end crew is a culinary artist who mans the coal stove and takes care of the cooking. On some roads, conductors are assigned regular cabooses, and it is not uncommon for a caboose to have lace curtains, framed pictures, chairs, and soft mattresses—with white linen and bedspreads! Now, during the war, the cabooses are usually assigned to a pool that remains on a certain run (or *division*). The dial above the conductor's head in the picture opposite is the air gauge; by pulling the nearby valve, air can be "dumped" to set the train's brakes in an emergency. (DELANO)

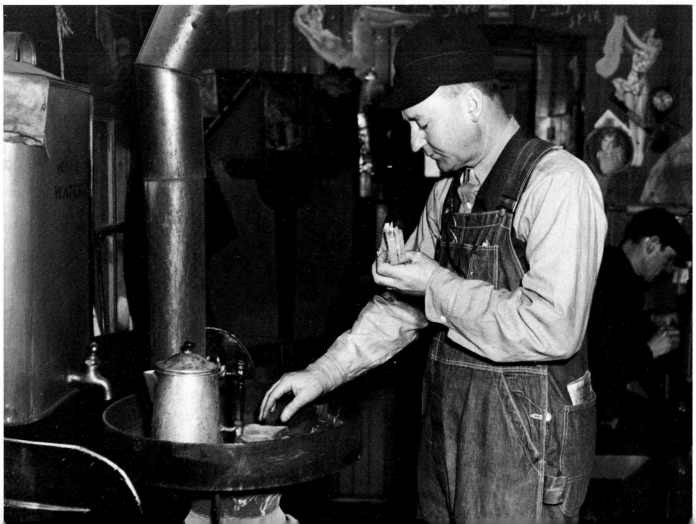

The commonly used term *manifest* should be explained—especially since we're riding one! The term simply means fast freight, and depending on the railroad, a manifest may also be called a *hotshot,* a *preference freight,* a *redball,* or a *symbol train.* Its consist may include livestock, perishables, or general merchandise. During the war, oil trains and coal trains sometimes move as manifests, and so, of course, do all military freight trains that are "permitted fast running."

Many, many hours and many, many miles have passed, and we're nearing our destination. We're on time. No stops, no delays—the way the dispatcher and everyone on the railroad wants it: "Clear" on the home-board. On the head end, the fireman watches the lurking dwarf signals and calls the signals out to the engineer. The hogger works the air, holding the train in check, slowing for the yard limit. Back in the caboose, the brake reduction is felt through the train's slack; the steely brakeshoe smoke is now very evident throughout the caboose. At left, above, the flagman gets out a fusee to protect the train in case a stop is necessary before getting into the yard. Once the train is stopped (below), the markers are removed from the rear of the caboose and new markers are set on the other end. The switch engine will couple on and back us off the hind end of our train.

One of the most important rules of the railroad is that at the end of the run trainmen, enginemen, and conductors must examine the superintendent's bulletins and notices before concluding each day's work. After that is done the crew will register out, for ten hours off before the next tour of duty. Opposite, the road engine has been cut off and heads toward the roundhouse for servicing. (DELANO)

Not every train is a main train or a manifest train; not every train is rushed along behind a huge fast-stepping locomotive, either, as is commonly envisioned. During the grain harvest in our breadbasket states, the boxcar is as vital to the movement of the harvest as it is to the movement of military goods. The three railroad scenes on these pages certainly don't convey any feeling of urgency, but don't be mistaken—the grain rush is on! Solid boxcar trains filled with wheat are being rushed to the flour mills at Minneapolis and to scores of other midwestern flour hubs, as well as to storage elevators throughout the land—and the rush is also on to get the empties *back* to the elevator sidings for reloading. Barley, oats, rye, corn, flaxseed, and sugar beets are joining the wheat, riding the rails. Whatever the harvest—rice from Louisiana, apples from Oregon, shrimp from Mississippi, grapefruit from Florida, or dates from California—the railroads are handling everything in stride. Food keeps the home front going! Food keeps the GI's going! (DELANO)

The conductors and enginemen may *run* the trains, but it is the dispatcher who *directs* the trains' movements, working closely with the operators out on the line. For operating purposes, every railroad is made up of segments called *blocks,* each under the direct charge of an operator (or *agent-operator,* as he is sometimes called). The operator is in constant telephone contact with the dispatcher, who schedules all trains to proceed, meet, pass, and arrive according to his orders. When a train passes an operator, he writes down the engine number, train direction, and time, and notifies the dispatcher and the next block operator who will be handling the train. The operator must report any improper display of engine or rear-end markers and must carefully inspect the passing train, looking for any sign of trouble. The dispatcher, talking to operators and working from his train sheet, watches the whole division at work—from his desk. When specific instructions need to be issued to train crews, the operator (above) copies the orders from the dispatcher and "hands them up" to the train crews, using an order hoop (opposite). On the railroad it's said, "You can't learn to be a dispatcher—you must be born one!" (YOUNG, HASTINGS, COLLECTION)

173

The best locomotives, cars, signals, and operating personnel in the world aren't worth a fig without good track. The Maintenance of Way Department has the responsibility of keeping the track, bridges, and buildings in good condition. Every railroad is composed of several divisions, which are usually made up of districts, each of which has several sections. Every section is assigned a section foreman who knows his part of the railroad—in his sleep!

Above, the section foreman, or "boss," gets his track in line on the inside of a curve. This is also done with the aid of a board—which a good section boss doesn't need. Opposite, two track workers tighten the bolts on a crossover, or "diamond," between the tracks of two railroads. A long, heavy freight train traveling at moderate to high speed can shake these bolts loose as it clatters over the diamond. Crossovers must be checked constantly. (HASTINGS, COOK)

The war has had its effect on every aspect of railroading. Never overlook the fact that the railroad is an integral part of the Post Office Department—performing the duty of delivering the mail and express. Almost in proportion to the military traffic, the volume of mail and express handled by the railroads has *doubled* in a little over a year after Pearl Harbor. To handle this growth of military mail, both domestic and for shipment overseas, great increases in the labor force and equipment have been made.

Small towns located in the proximity of a base—especially the ones with one Railway Express agent and one baggage wagon—have been hit harder, proportionately, by the increased mail than the large cities. Above: the grand old game "How high can I pile it?"—and left, the Railway Express driver and agent look on with uncertainty at the artistry of the baggageman topping the bags window high. Opposite: a quiet moment on the railroad—a few minutes to chat before rolling the wagon across to the other platform. (DELANO, DELANO, NOWAK)

Watches, signals, and tracks have to be maintained to keep the railroad the smooth-running artery that's so necessary in the war effort. Few laymen realize how important time is to the railroader—right down to the second. An operating employee's watch must not vary more than *thirty seconds* from the official standard time *over a period of a week!* A rule of the railroad is that all crew members must wind their watches so they run at least sixteen hours before the start of each trip. Employees are cautioned not to set their watches—that delicate task is assigned only to watch inspectors. Before starting the work day or a trip, time comparison must be made among crew members who must have previously checked with one of the railroad's standard clocks. Any discrepancy must be reported to the nearest watch inspector (above).

At right, signal maintainers relax during a heavy traffic peak on a routine check of the signal system. The important task of seeing that the signals are in order necessitates that these men be "detectives," mechanics, and electricians. The signal department of the railroad also maintains the dwarf signals, train signs, switch indicators, speed-limit boards, and interlocking signals. Opposite, the foreman supervises a track gang laying down the longer crossover tracks required by the larger locomotives now being delivered to the railroad. (NOWAK, DONAHUE, NOWAK)

178

A tower operator at a busy junction has his work cut out for him, performing a multitude of duties; operators are responsible for arranging the use of blocks, tracks, interlockings, switches, and signals in accordance with the rules, train orders, and special instructions.

T&NO Junction and Tower 81, four miles out of Houston's busy Union Station, is a typical "hot spot" on the railroad where a single operator handles each and every train passing through the junction. As the trains "hit the bell" and clatter over the diamond, the operator throws a multitude of switch levers, keeping the moving trains on the right track. Come to think of it, like the dispatcher, maybe one has to be *born* a tower operator! (HASTINGS)

From Pearl Harbor to the end of June 1945, the railroads handled more than 278,000,000 tons of freight for the Army. In March 1945 alone, the railroads handled a greater volume of matériel for the European front than was moved in the entire period of U.S. participation in the First World War—and they did it with 600,000 fewer freight cars and 22,000 fewer locomotives! From December 1941 to June 1945, 39,200,000 troops were carried by train in organized movements—not including several million traveling under orders in smaller groups or the members of the Allied armies and navies traveling in the United States. And these figures do not include the millions of soldiers, sailors, and members of women's service units traveling on furlough or weekend passes—they cover only the military moves; the nation's railroads were meanwhile busy taking care of civilians, too. Perhaps we now understand a little better that the railroads were indeed doing the impossible, all the time! (DELANO, DELANO, BALL)

4

THE STATION AND THE DEPOT

THE FRENCH CONTRIBUTED to the American language not only terms for the arts of war, but also the word for an institution once as conspicuous a part of the culture of the United States as the fast-food enterprise is today: that word is *depot*. Elaborations and variations on the theme of depot adorned the center of every village and town that lay along the right-of-way of the railways as they reached farther and farther inland. The depot was the focus of the community: everything came there first—people, goods, the daily newspapers, the daily mail, the telegrams—and the lord of that manor, the station-master, ranked in social standing and in prominence with the town councilmen or even the mayor.

In the quarter-century that preceded the Second World War, there was a slow wasting away of this one-time town social center, but at the beginning of the war there were still examples enough to serve properly the depot's existing functions and also the new functions that it would be called upon to perform with efficiency in wartime. Baggage rooms that might have lain empty for years now became repositories for the apparatus of the Red Cross can-

teens. The scent of warm doughnuts and hot coffee enriched the middle of the night at station after station at which troop trains paused—even when, by order, the soldiers should have been long abed.

The stations, the terminals, of the great railways were social centers of another sort in the cities. South Station in Boston offered one of the best seafood restaurants in that city; Grand Central Terminal in New York offered the Oyster Bar, a restaurant favored by nearly everyone who passed through town. (In a rare reversal of current trends, the Oyster Bar has lately been lifted to heights hitherto unattained.) In Philadelphia there was a reasonably grandiose counterpart: the dining room in the lamented, now-lost temple known as Broad Street Station was one of the best in the city.

The most celebrated of all American railway caterers was Fred Harvey, whose genteel Harvey Girls once staffed the station restaurants along the main lines of the Santa Fe. He lent his name to a fleet of little gourmet palaces that spread as far east as Union Terminal in Cleveland. In Kansas City's Union Station, the Westport Room of the Fred Harvey restaurant was set aside on New Year's Eve for black-tie parties.

One dined in style in those early railway restaurants. In the Spanish Colonial reaches of Los Angeles Union Passenger Terminal, one dined at Spanish Colonial leisure; in the Lackawanna Terminal in Hoboken, New Jersey, one ate shad roe from the Hudson—pre-pollution days—that was not to be surpassed; in San Francisco, in the Southern Pacific's engaging little station at Third and Townsend streets, the jolliest, the friendliest assortment of commuters in the United States gathered at Rickey's Bar well in advance of their trains heading down the Peninsula.

And what better witness to a salient truth—that Chicago is the railway center of the United States— than its Union Station? In the 1940s Chicago was as rich in railway stations as London remains today, and Union's rivals were worthy satellites—in particular the Illinois Central's monumental manse, the Baltimore & Ohio's grandiose counterpart (with its stately porte-cochere), and Dearborn Street Station (with its ascending-to-heaven spires)—but none approached Union's lordly expanses of vaulted spaces, of classic staircases and balustrades, of shops and restaurants and bars, of marble, of architectural formalism, of architectural exuberance.

In the months just before our entrance into the Second World War, Union Station was already the teeing-off point for trains to cities all over the East, the South, the Midwest, the Southwest, the Northwest, and California. Its ground plan, well laid out for the purpose at hand (in unconscious preparation for the wartime flood), was unique: a stub terminal on the north side for trains of the Milwaukee Road; a stub terminal on the south side for the trains of the Burlington (now the Burlington Northern), the Pennsylvania (now under the umbrella of the federal government's Conrail system), and the Alton (which later became part of the Gulf, Mobile & Ohio, and still later part of the Illinois Central Gulf); and a set of tracks running north and south straight through the station's east side. The through tracks, already useful for the transferring of baggage, mail, and express cars from the three railways on the south side to the Milwaukee Road on the north, became even more useful for the through-running of troops during the war; in the postwar years, during the brief but glorious splurge of coast-to-coast sleeping-car runs,

these tracks made transferring through sleepers from train to train a task of almost ridiculous simplicity. Only one other such railway station exists, as globe-roving railway buffs know—the Hauptbahnhof in Dresden, East Germany.

A typical morning early in May 1941, when assiduous American railway buffs are still more concerned with traveling and observing than with thoughts of military service, finds a group of young men on the south stub platforms of Union Station, notebooks in hand. (Cameras are already objects of alarm; the threatening war and premonitions of saboteurs have made railroad managements reluctant to allow photographing at will in stations, but a few young men wandering among the commuters on the Burlington's local services are not likely to draw attention.)

One of these buffs has decided to spend an exhausting day of observation on the south platforms. He has recently graduated from Massachusetts Institute of Technology and has just finished a tour of duty in the Yale University School of Transportation. In a few weeks he will be going to work for the Missouri Pacific, as co-supervisor of a maintenance-of-way gang, along with the son of a chief executive of the New York Central. His new job is one in which many a young railway man has commenced his climb toward the upper echelons of railway management. Because he is a railway buff, he has not driven his car (a graduation gift from his family) from Lake Forest into town but has come down in an early Chicago & North Western commuter train, has walked the short distance to Union Station, and has had breakfast in the Fred Harvey restaurant. Because he is a conscientious buff, he will today stake out the south platforms and set down in his notebook the name or number of every departing longer-distance train, the details of its locomotives (he will ultimately conclude with regret that there are more diesels than when he came home at Christmastime), and the name and number of every car.

At 8:30 A.M. he makes his first notes—dealing with the departure of the Alton's *Ann Rutledge,* for Saint Louis, properly outfitted with dining car and parlors. At 8:55 he notes the Alton's maid-of-all-work—the Saint Louis local, far more concerned with the mail and express cars than it is with its passenger coaches; this train is an all-day dawdler. At 9:00 the

Burlington's *Morning Zephyr* is off for the Twin Cities—the young observer calls it "a tin can" (a low-slung, lightweight, aluminum-hued express)—even though it sports a dining car, a parlor car, and an observation car. Steam, at 9:30, takes the Pennsylvania *New Yorker* east; hung on the rear of it are the cars that will be detached at Fort Wayne, Indiana, to become the *Detroit Express,* which will depart thence over the Wabash.

Every third day (and this is the third day), the Pennsylvania's *South Wind* goes out for Florida. It has a "de-luxe" listing in the timetables, and it deserves this rating. At 9:45 the Pennsy sends south its *Fort Hayes*—part of it for Louisville, part of it for Columbus. At 10:15 the Burlington's maid-of-all-work, the *Overland,* some of whose consist will end up in California, sets out for Omaha. At 10:30 the Milwaukee's maid-of-all-work—mail and express cars, plus a brace of coaches—takes off for the Twin Cities. At 11:00 A.M. the Pennsy's *Manhattan Limited,* a well-upholstered express for New York, is under way. At 11:40 the *Alton Limited* is away for Saint Louis, with a Pullman sleeper that will spend the night on the Frisco en route to Oklahoma City.

The Santa Fe and the Union Pacific are, in that order, the major carriers to the central and southern West Coast, but the Burlington offers a fine challenger—the 12:35 P.M. *Exposition Flyer,* which does the run to Oakland, California, the hardest way: through the middle of the Rockies; this day its solarium observation car bears the name "Burlington Route," though the Burlington takes it no farther west than Denver. In later years, on the advice of Gilbert Kneiss of the Western Pacific, this express will become the *California Zephyr,* a streamlined paragon whose amenities will make it one of the world's most famous trains. So heavily laden is the *Flyer* today that a second section must be run, all the way to Lincoln, Nebraska; such sections are often needed.

Fifteen minutes later, at 12:50, the Pennsy's *Flamingo* gets under way for Florida; she is coupled to Pennsy's *Union,* which splits two ways—one part for Cincinnati, one part for Columbus. It is a bit of a puzzle, this train, for the unknowing traveler; railway buffs know precisely how it works. At 1:30 the Pennsy's new experiment to win the overnight bus travelers back to the railways, the *Trail Blazer*—with the very best of reserved-seat coaches, a club

car, a dining car, an observation car, a running time of only seventeen hours and a fare of only $18.20 (two cents a mile)—is en route to New York and Washington. An hour later, the Pennsy's *Advance General*—a sizable wake of Pullman sleeping cars in its consist—follows suit. The *Advance General*—and the *General,* soon to follow—are named for General W. W. Atterbury, under whose leadership the Pennsylvania attained a level of performance that gave it fair claim to its chosen title "Standard Railroad of the World." At 3:30 the Pennsy's *Liberty Limited,* due in Washington the next morning, is off and running. Ten minutes after her, the Burlington's shining "tin can" *Afternoon Zephyr* is off on its way to the Twin Cities; alongside the *Zephyr,* the *General* is away for New York at the same moment—this train is second in appointments only to the Pennsy's *Broadway Limited.*

At 4:15 the Pennsy's *Detroit Arrow,* which this afternoon is sporting on its rear end the "Queen Mary," Pennsy's most celebrated observation/parlor car, rolls away toward Fort Wayne and the Wabash route to Michigan. Even with a call at Englewood, the "uptown" station in Chicago, the K-4 on the end of the *Arrow* will wheel its load into Fort Wayne, 148 miles away, in a mere 128 minutes. To the young observer in Union Station, this train's departure is the pinnacle of his day, even though a quarter of an hour later the Pennsy's *Broadway Limited*—with a mail car, fifteen sleepers, a dining car, an observation Pullman, and not a single day coach—departs on the sixteen-hour run to New York (the 1977 timing will be almost nineteen hours). At 4:50 the Alton's *Abraham Lincoln,* its showpiece of the day, tools south for Saint Louis, and ten minutes later the Pennsy's *Rainbow* begins its journey to New York. At 5:30 the Burlington's *Denver Zephyr,* another "tin can," but one equipped with a galaxy of sleeping cars and an observation sleeper that affords the most spacious drawing room in this part of the world, takes off for the West.

Time out, now, for the observer to have a small dinner in the Golden Lion, Fred Harvey's most prestigious sector of the dining accommodations in Union Station. Then back on point duty along the south platforms, for at 6:30 the Burlington's *Ak-Sar-Ben* departs, with sleeping cars not only for Omaha and Lincoln, but also for Saint Joseph, Missouri, and Kansas City (this means a problem of—shall we say?—"long division" in the middle of the night). Fifteen minutes more, and an Alton run to Saint Louis—a secondary train entitled simply the *Mail*—pulls out of town. One of its sleepers will go on past Saint Louis to Hot Springs, Arkansas; the other will be detached at Bloomington, Illinois, 127 miles away, to be placed aboard the *Hummer,* the Alton's around-Robin-Hood's-barn run to Kansas City.

At 8:00 the Pennsy's *Pennsylvania Limited,* its sleepers filled mainly by late arrivals from the north and the west, makes its departure for New York. At 9:00 the Burlington's *Fast Mail,* whose run ends at Lincoln, is ready; much of its mail and express will be transferred along the way to a battalion of Burlington branch-line mixed trains. At 9:20 sleeping cars roll south toward Cincinnati in a Pennsy express, and at 10:00 P.M. the Burlington's *Black Hawk* commences its overnight (sleeping-car) run to the Twin Cities. At 10:15 another exercise in long division leaves—the Pennsy's *Gotham Limited* for New York; hours later it will shed the part of its consist called the *Valley Special,* which delivers sleeping-car passengers to a string of mid-Ohio industrial cities and even pokes its nose as far north (roundabout fashion) as Cleveland.

At 11:00 the Burlington's splendid *North Coast Limited,* destination the Pacific Northwest, pushes off, just as the Pennsy's overnight run to Pittsburgh, the *Golden Triangle,* well equipped with sleeping cars, is off. Ten minutes to go, now, for a Pennsy night express, the *Ohioan,* whose destination is Cincinnati. The Burlington's *Empire Builder,* which ranks among the best services in the country—and whose route takes it through the Dakotas on a course quite different from the *North Coast Limited*'s route to Seattle—leaves next, five minutes later. Another five minutes, and the Pennsy's night train for Indianapolis and Louisville, with sleepers destined to both these cities, pulls away. Ten minutes after that, the Burlington's *Overland*—a leisurely night crawler that will deliver sleeping-car passengers to Kansas City and Saint Joseph in the morning—departs, and at that moment the Alton weighs in with its own *Fast Mail,* which will set out one sleeping car in Springfield, Illinois, and deposit another at the end of the run, Saint Louis. At 11:40 the Pennsy's *Southland,* the last of the day's Florida trains, leaves, to go east as far as Fort Wayne before it turns south—more sleeping cars. At 11:50 the

Pennsy's *Mid-City Express* moves out, with a few sleepers, on the Fort Wayne-Wabash run to Detroit. At 11:59 P.M. the Alton's principal night train to Saint Louis, which skips most of the calls the Alton's *Fast Mail* makes, is away. Our observer's turn of duty has ended.

A vigil this same day in 1941 by a different observer—on the north platforms of Union Station—is also richly rewarded, but only one railway, the Milwaukee Road, is involved. There is a considerable ebb and flow of commuting services, and with the departures and arrivals of the Milwaukee's long-distance trains, the traffic attains most respectable proportions. These departures begin at 8:10 A.M. with an express to Milwaukee, outfitted—like almost every express anywhere in the United States on a daytime run—with a parlor car. At 9:10 another express, similarly outfitted, heads toward Milwaukee, and at 9:15 there's an express to Madison, also with parlor car. At 9:45 Milwaukee's justifiable pride, the *Morning Hiawatha,* departs for the Twin Cities—wholly streamlined, with the speed of the wind and all the amenities the exacting traveler considers a matter of course in 1941. At 12:45 P.M. the *Mid-West Hiawatha* takes off, to divide, halfway across Iowa, into sections (both with a parlor car) for Omaha and Sioux Falls, South Dakota. (The *Mid-West Hiawatha,* fine train though it was, never aroused as much enthusiasm—or custom—as its Twin Cities counterparts, the *Morning* and *Afternoon Hiawatha*s, but the Milwaukee Road maintained its high standards, perhaps rejoicing over the line's graduation from a long-term bankruptcy, determined to afford its patrons the best of everything, everywhere.) At 1:00 the second Twin Cities flyer, the *Afternoon Hiawatha,* quite as grand as the earlier one, is away. (It is worth noting that there may be an unrecorded gentlemen's agreement between the two major carriers on the run between Chicago and the Twin Cities; the Burlington and the Milwaukee do, in fact, space out the departure times of their expresses on that route so well that the danger of sending out two half-empty trains simultaneously is avoided—a reasonable managerial precaution.) A change of trains at Milwaukee puts some of the *Afternoon Hiawatha*'s passengers aboard the Milwaukee *Chippewa*—again with parlor car—heading for Green Bay, then on to the Upper Michigan Peninsula and up through its iron-mining country to Ontonagon, the jumping-off place for resort country. Two hours out of Milwaukee, closing in on the Twin Cities, the *Afternoon Hiawatha* stops and yields passengers to another train, the *North Woods Hiawatha,* waiting to originate at New Lisbon, Wisconsin; with a solarium parlor on the back end, the latter train heads for a few big paper-manufacturing cities in Wisconsin and then for that state's holiday territory. The *Hiawathas* are always decorated at the rear with the "beavertail" observation car that makes them both celebrated and distinctive.

Now the observer has an ample lunch, as always at a Fred Harvey table in Union Station, before the next departure of interest—the 3:45, which will split at Milwaukee into two portions, a parlor car in each consist: one for Madison and one for Green Bay. At 6:50 a flurry of outbound expresses commences. First off is a parlor-car run to Madison. Five minutes later comes the *Sioux,* which, hauling its solitary sleeping car all the way west, will not finish its journey to Rapid City, South Dakota, until the second morning. True railway buffs deem the *Sioux* the most hallowed of all local trains. Passengers in the drawing room of its Pullman relax and consider the evening scenery from whatever seats are available in the Madison parlor car, then withdraw to a café car for dinner. At Mason City, Iowa, one of the principal stops en route, another café car is attached, around four o'clock next morning; they can breakfast in it until 9:30, when the train reaches Canton, a junction just across the South Dakota border. There the café car and the solarium parlor car that was also added at Mason City are detached and joined to a different train that takes a tangent northward to the considerable town of Sioux Falls. Passengers staying aboard the *Sioux* for Rapid City have to catch breakfast before the train arrives at Canton or else for another entire day live off the country—digesting its picturesque and unique Badland territory.

Twenty-five minutes after the *Sioux* moves out, the *Arrow* sets forth west, with dining-car service all the way and with sleeping cars for Sioux Falls, Omaha, Des Moines, and Sioux City, Iowa. On its many-pronged journey it will collect from a branch-line train one sleeping car that will run from Milwaukee to Omaha; from another branch-line train, a sleeping car for the Des Moines–Sioux City stretch. A Pullman lounge car out of Chicago even offers a valet. Five minutes after the *Arrow* leaves Union

Station, the northbound *Copper Country Limited* rolls away. This operation, not quite as complex as the *Arrow,* follows the *Chippewa's* track even farther north than Ontonagon, to the very tip of the upper Michigan Peninsula—the copper-mining city of Calumet. There is a Calumet sleeping car and an Iron River sleeping car; another sleeping car is removed at a junction around three in the morning, sits on a siding for three hours, and then turns at right angles east on a Soo Line local and drifts into Sault Sainte Marie, across the straits from western Ontario, at 1:45 P.M.

A pause in northbound departures, now, until 9:15, when a parlor-car train bound for Madison sets off. The dining car in the *Pioneer Limited* has already opened, at 9:00, though the *Pioneer* is not due away until 10:15. Some of the Milwaukee Road's own (that is, not Pullman) sleeping cars, with their seven-foot-long berths, have not yet been put out to pasture; several of them may be in the *Pioneer* consist, to the delight of connoisseurs. The *Pioneer* is held to be *the* overnight train to the Twin Cities, no matter what the competing Chicago & North Western, Soo Line, and Burlington offer, just as the *Twentieth-Century Limited* is held to be *the* overnight train between Chicago and New York, no matter what the opposition may offer—principally the *Broadway Limited.* (The *Broadway* will survive into the 1970s, in somewhat subdued array, but the *Pioneer* and the *Century* will have become memories by then.)

At 10:45 it is time for the *Marquette,* one more Milwaukee Road express with a split personality—a sleeper for Mason City (arriving at a more reasonable hour than the *Sioux*) and sleeping cars to the Twin Cities by a roundabout route that goes far west of the Milwaukee Road's main line. At 11:15 the *Olympian* (which takes its name from the Olympic Peninsula, just across the water from Seattle), is on its way to the Pacific Northwest—a train so attuned to the niceties of civilization that every afternoon it serves tea formally to its Pullman passengers in the observation car, awarding daily, to the young lady who volunteers to pour, a set of Milwaukee Road china.

Bedtime now, except for anyone who wishes to wait up for the 1:15 A.M. mail, whose nearly-all-stations run to the Twin Cities is a weary one for the inhabitants of its two day coaches.

This, then, was the day's work that spring day in

Union Station, and apart from a few alterations in schedules, it was still the day's work on December 7, 1941. There were trains enough, and rolling stock enough, to get anyone nearly anywhere, and there was a capacity to expand almost infinitely when the burden of the war descended upon the railways.

But for every station like Union in Chicago or Grand Central in New York or South Station in Boston, or Union in Dallas or Union in Denver or Union in Los Angeles, there were hundreds of minor outposts—some of incredible loneliness. . . .

Out of Tucumcari, New Mexico—a town busy beyond belief with military traffic, for it is the junction of the Rock Island and the Southern Pacific—a Southern Pacific branch runs north through country dubious in summer and hazardous in winter. It ends at Dawson, New Mexico, where mining activities are in decline. The branch is one that the Office of Defense Transportation might well consider closing, if it were not that along the route, in bleakest desert, is a plant that extracts from beneath the surface of the land a gas that is an important ingredient in making dry ice—and dry ice is an important commodity in wartime.

The solitary train that works from Tucumcari to Dawson sets out and picks up tank cars at the dry-ice plant, and, since public transport is even scarcer than people in this desolate territory, it carries what few passengers there are in its caboose. Several miles south of Dawson, the line crosses, on a wooden trestle, the main line of the Santa Fe between Chicago and California. The train then backs down a steep spur to the Santa Fe station—which is a one-room hut, without an agent.

On a normal day, the conductor of the Southern Pacific train unfastens the padlock on the door, enters to sign the train register, locks up, and waves his train off for Dawson. On this two-degrees-above-zero February morning in 1943, however, he is followed into this station (French, New Mexico, is its name, if that matters) by a passenger who boarded at the dry-ice plant—a sudden illness in his family is calling him home. So on this day the conductor of the Southern Pacific train shoves some newspaper and several sticks of wood into the stove in the middle of the room and lights a fire. There will be a Santa Fe passenger train of no special importance bound east in a couple of hours, if it is on schedule—which is not the rule with less important trains during a world war. It is the only eastbound Santa Fe train that calls at French, and it calls only on signal. There is a woodbox out back of the station, in case the passenger needs a warmer fire. What little there is of the hamlet of French looks snowbound, and more snow comes down as the conductor bids farewell, boards his train, and departs for Dawson, leaving the station padlock lying on the bench. The traveler has been instructed to pull a handle attached to a vertical wire that will operate a signal board on top of a pole, thus telling the engineer of the eastbound Santa Fe train that, after a lapse of four months, a passenger is waiting at French. After he is certain that the engineer has seen the signal, the passenger will maneuver the signal board out of position, close the door of the station, snap the padlock shut, and be on his way east a minute or two later. Can French, New Mexico, be the loneliest railway station on the North American continent? The solitary passenger, who has to wait 4½ hours before the engineer acknowledges the signal board with his locomotive whistle, decides that it is.

First and second sections of *Denver Zephyr* backing into
Chicago Union Station, 1943. (COLLECTION)

The opening years of the twentieth century were a great period of growth and expansion for the railroads. Dynamic, highly able, and ambitious men were building the railroads, and their own railroad empires. Overnight, the bigger, more prosperous roads swallowed up the smaller lines, establishing their root system from city to city. The station became the symbol of—indeed, the monument to—the railroad and its achievement. In many a city, the railroads collectively built a magnificent passenger station, and for years it would remain the gate to the city.

Chicago's Union Station was officially opened in July 1925, and was hailed as America's latest triumph in railroading. The Chicago Union Station Company had been incorporated to build the station in 1913 by the Chicago, Burlington & Quincy, the Chicago, Milwaukee, St. Paul & Pacific, and the Pennsylvania Railroad; the Chicago & Alton remained a tenant. We will spend part of a day at Union Station; the date—January 15, 1943.

Opposite, the midday sun streams into the huge waiting room—269 feet long, 100 feet wide, 111 feet high. Above: the station clock, and the neon-brass-paint-and-chalk train arrival board. (DELANO)

The January 1926 issue of *Western Architect* said that the interior handling of Union Station's 192-by-203-foot concourse was its most "interesting feature," describing its steel inner structure as "web-like, aspiring, latticed columns which rise from the floor in a sheer and stalwart fashion to bear aloft a beautifully graceful segmented roof."

All day long this concourse echoes with the din of hurrying feet; beyond the gates, the trains arrive and depart to the cadence of rumbling wheels, hissing steam, and tolling bells. Announcements of departures and arrivals ring throughout the cavernous station. In just twenty-four hours, close to three hundred in- and outbound trains will rattle over the 24 tracks leading to the north and south sides of the concourse! (DELANO)

As war traffic peaks, over a million GI's are being moved every month over America's railroads. This figure swells considerably when the Navy, Coast Guard, and Marines are added, along with the numerous "casual" groups of fewer than fifty men. Each service has an organization set up to work with the railroads. The Army troop movements originate with the General Staff; all details are channeled down to the Passenger Branch/Traffic Control Division of the Transportation Corps, which works closely with the Military Transportation Section of the Association of American Railroads (AAR). The Military Transportation Section then gives the railways involved the equipment requirements, origins, and destination of the moves. The Pullman Company will also be advised when sleepers are required. *The Transportation Corps is in charge of the troop train from the time it starts until it reaches its destination.* Each railroad handles requests and equipment assignments through its military bureau, making cooperation with the military the highest priority. When groups of forty-nine or fewer men are involved in a move, the local transportation officer makes the arrangements for regular train accommodations, reporting all details to the Military Transportation Section of the AAR.

Above, military and civilians wait in line for their reservations and Pennsylvania Railroad trains; opposite, soldiers who have completed their basic training get ready to board a Burlington extra to an assembly point at Camp Grant, from which they will depart for camps, bases—and trenches—overseas. (DELANO)

When individual soldiers or small groups receive their orders, the railway military bureaus determine which railroads and routes the soldiers will travel, trying always to give all carriers their proportionate share of the traffic. This is accomplished with so-called period routing orders, under which all individuals and small groups move over specified routes and railroads between specified dates. At the expiration of the period designated, the routes are switched back to a competing line. This arrangement helps balance the load—and the share of the business—between carriers, and at the same time allows for orderly planning of maintenance and the handling of large-scale movements of troops and matériel.

Pictured on this spread are the usual activities (besides selling railroad and Pullman tickets) of a large ticket office—from checking schedules and quoting rates, to pulling reservations, checking accommodations, and calling connecting railroads. (DELANO)

The hour draws near, and the last few precious moments of weekend furlough come to an end. For many, the parting will be for many, many months; for some, forever.

When a group or detachment is not large enough to justify a special train back to a base—as is usually the case with weekend furloughs—extra cars are usually attached to a regular train. Each soldier is allowed a one-dollar meal in the dining car, and most dining-car stewards prepare special "GI dinners." If a soldier wants something other than the special, a dollar will be credited to his check. In troop trains, however, the boys go to the kitchen car with their mess kits to get their grub. All the coffee, milk, and soft drinks that anyone cares to drink are available at all times on a troop train. "The American army travels on its stomach," and travels very well! (DELANO)

Though thousands of miles from the bombing, America's involvement in the war is very real at home. From assembly lines to War Bonds, from Civil Defense to Victory Gardens and gasoline rationing, no one for a moment forgets that the nation is at war! Patriotic posters, advertisements, and slogans are ever present, constantly bringing the message home. On these pages, appropriate posters and slogans adorn each end of the immense main concourse at Union Station. (DELANO)

Beyond the gates, the tracks come in from the south and the north, terminating at both sides of the station. The Burlington, the Pennsylvania, and the Chicago & Alton use the south wing; the Milwaukee uses the north. The trains on these pages depict the head-end power of the three roads that tie up on the south end.

At left, the fireman off Alton's *Abraham Lincoln* climbs down from B&O diesel No. 50 after the last passenger has headed to the gate. B&O's pioneer passenger diesels often worked on the B&O-controlled Alton Railroad, between St. Louis and Chicago, and sometimes between west-to-east runs on the B&O, too. Below, the last passengers off Burlington's streamlined *Denver Zephyr* head for the station and the pleasures of its Roman Corinthian and Italian travertine decor. Opposite, the wind and snow whip through the Bush-style smoke openings over the tracks, pushing the steam down over the streamlined flanks of Pennsy's rakish T-1 steam duplex No. 6110. These three locomotives have brought the term *streamliner* to America's railroads—and to the American consciousness. (DELANO)

"Classic contrasts between stainless and steam." At left, Pennsy's standard K-4 No. 5493 in from the East with the *Pennsylvania Limited,* pants to a stop beyond the *Denver Zephyr.* Below, the engineer off the *Limited* reports the condition of his engine to the inspector—but not before getting in a few quips. Opposite, between runs, brakemen off the four railroads serving Union Station relax over poker and share thoughts in the brakeman's locker and rest room. (DELANO)

The marvel of Chicago's Union Station is the fact that it is really under the control of *one man*—a man to whom it is as simple as the ten fingers of his hands. The head man in the tower is the chief towerman, and along with his assistants, he commands and controls all the switches and protecting signals in and out of Union Station from a central console, the interlocking machine (opposite). The levers in the tower are controlled so that signals cannot be given for trains to proceed until all switches in the route governed are first properly set and locked; conversely, the switches of a route governed by signal cannot be moved during the display or signal giving the right of way over them. Hanging above the interlocking machine is an illuminated panel that displays train locations and track alignments.

At right, the official watch inspector's office at the south end of the station, where railroad men have their watches periodically inspected and certified. Below, the Pennsylvania Railroad section of the reservation bureau at Union Station. Union, like most other large stations, is a city unto itself, maintaining a seventeen-man police force, a volunteer fire department, a nursery, and two small hospitals—along with all the other services required by its patrons. (DELANO)

The constant parade of trains departing Union Station slams out from under the Post Office building and past the tower, heading out of town. Above, two of Pennsy's magnificent K-4's wham away at Harrison Street and into the sun, hammering through the interlocking with the heavy second section of the *Fort Pitt*. At right, the clean-fired K-4's blast by, gaining on the departing *South Wind* and its streamlined K-4. Opposite, Alton's beautiful Pacific No. 5273 heads train #11 out of Union under its billowing plume of steam, while to the right, a Pennsy B-6 switcher pulls the now-empty *Broadway Limited* out from its stub track, en route to the nearby coach yard. (DELANO)

Below, another quick look at Alton's loud-talking Pacific No. 5273 stepping through the turnouts on its way toward St. Louis; the straining B-6 with its trailing *Broadway Limited* cars is now under way. Opposite, Burlington's *Afternoon Zephyr* growls out from under the cavernous environs of Union and the Post Office building, en route to St. Paul and Minneapolis. The gleaming power on the head end is E-5 diesel "Silver Meteor" and mate "Silver Comet." (DELANO)

New York City's Penn Station was completed on November 27, 1910, and was the largest structure in the world devoted solely to use by railroad passengers. Into its construction went 550,000 cubic feet of granite, 27,000 tons of steel, and 15,000,000 bricks. To support the station, 650 great columns, some weighing as much as 1,658 tons, were used! Inspired by the great buildings of ancient Rome—particularly the Baths of Caracalla, of Titus, and of Diocletian, and the Basilica of Constantine—it cost $125 million to build. In terms of cost and the size of the task, this construction job was second only to the building of the Panama Canal!

Above: the glass and steel latticework patterns of the domelike roof over the train concourse. At right: the main entrance, reminiscent of the Brandenburg Gate in Berlin, is adorned with fourteen sandstone American eagles, each one weighing close to three tons! Opposite: the passenger concourse and one of its seven-foot clocks. In 1945, 109 million passengers traveled over Penn Station's twenty-one tracks and more than five miles of platforms, and—in all likelihood—most passed through its huge (150 feet high, 277 feet long, 103 feet wide) main waiting room. (BALL, BALL, PRINT COLLECTION)

Grand Central Terminal—"Gateway to a Continent"—is considered by many to be New York City's most beautiful edifice, and it is certainly the most handsome and most efficient large station the railroad age ever produced. Spreading over a forty-eight-acre site in the heart of Manhattan, the terminal has, in addition to its railroad facilities, a hospital, an art gallery, several restaurants, and numerous shops and stores. Three major hotels have direct entrances into the terminal. The New York Central and the New York, New Haven & Hartford use the 48 platform tracks, of which 11 are connected with loops for turning trains and 37 are stub end. There are also numerous ladder tracks and storage tracks—for a total of 123 tracks in the terminal!

Opposite: the sculpture atop the terminal by Jules Coutan, featuring Hercules, Mercury, and Minerva arranged around a 13-foot-high clock. Below: the view up Park and Vanderbilt avenues, which lead to the beaux-arts-style terminal. Over its main entrance is an inscription: TO THOSE WHO WITH HEAD, HEART AND HAND TOILED IN THE CONSTRUCTION OF THIS MONUMENT TO THE PUBLIC SERVICE, THIS IS INSCRIBED. At right, above and below: two views of "the most beautiful room in the world," Grand Central Terminal's main concourse—275 feet long, 125 feet wide, and 125 feet high. Overhead, the heavens reign—2,500 stars painted in gold leaf on a field of cerulean blue, plus sixty illuminated stars. Commodore Vanderbilt, we thank you! (Left page, BALL; right page, NOWAK)

"LEST WE FORGET"

ON APRIL 11, 1917, FIVE DAYS AFTER THE UNITED STATES ENTERED THE
WORLD WAR, REPRESENTATIVES OF PRACTICALLY ALL THE RAILROADS
IN THE COUNTRY ASSEMBLED IN WASHINGTON IN RESPONSE TO AN
INVITATION FROM THE COUNCIL OF NATIONAL DEFENSE, EXTENDED
THROUGH DANIEL WILLARD, CHAIRMAN OF THE ADVISORY COMMISSION,
AND UNANIMOUSLY ADOPTED THE FOLLOWING RESOLUTION:

"THAT THE RAILROADS OF THE UNITED STATES, ACTING THROUGH THEIR
CHIEF EXECUTIVE OFFICERS HERE AND NOW ASSEMBLED, AND STIRRED
BY A HIGH SENSE OF THEIR OPPORTUNITY TO BE OF THE GREATEST
SERVICE TO THEIR COUNTRY IN THE PRESENT NATIONAL CRISIS, DO
HEREBY PLEDGE THEMSELVES, WITH THE GOVERNMENT OF THE UNITED
STATES, WITH THE GOVERNMENTS OF THE SEVERAL STATES, AND ONE
WITH ANOTHER, THAT DURING THE PRESENT WAR THEY WILL CO-ORDINATE
THEIR OPERATIONS IN A CONTINENTAL RAILWAY SYSTEM, MERGING
DURING SUCH PERIOD ALL THEIR MERELY INDIVIDUAL AND COMPETITIVE
ACTIVITIES IN THE EFFORT TO PRODUCE A MAXIMUM OF NATIONAL
TRANSPORTATION EFFICIENCY.   TO THIS END THEY HEREBY AGREE
TO CREATE AN ORGANIZATION WHICH SHALL HAVE GENERAL AUTHORITY
TO FORMULATE IN DETAIL AND FROM TIME TO TIME A POLICY OF
OPERATION OF ALL OR ANY OF THE RAILWAYS, WHICH POLICY, WHEN AND
AS ANNOUNCED BY SUCH TEMPORARY ORGANIZATION, SHALL BE ACCEPTED
AND EARNESTLY MADE EFFECTIVE BY THE SEVERAL MANAGEMENTS OF
THE INDIVIDUAL RAILROAD COMPANIES HERE REPRESENTED."

TO CARRY THIS PLEDGE INTO EFFECT, THE FOLLOWING EXECUTIVE
COMMITTEE WAS THAT DAY APPOINTED, WITH HEADQUARTERS IN
WASHINGTON:

FAIRFAX HARRISON, CHAIRMAN
PRESIDENT SOUTHERN RAILWAY

SAMUEL REA   JULIUS KRUTTSCHNITT
PRESIDENT PENNSYLVANIA RAILROAD   CHAIRMAN SOUTHERN PACIFIC

Beautiful Washington Union Station! Impressive from all angles, the station is an early example of the beaux arts style. Unlike many city stations, it is situated in a parklike setting, "unopposed" by nearby buildings. The grand entrance archways that rise up toward the barrel-vaulted roof over the waiting room are flanked with columns and statues. Farther back is the 760-foot-long concourse that leads to the trains. When completed in 1910, the majestic station had a separate entrance and waiting room for the President of the United States. During the Second World War, this private waiting room was given over to the USO. On December 23, 1945, over one hundred thousand people jammed onto the concourse—which only has a capacity of twenty-five thousand—and the station had to be closed until order could be restored!

On this spread are some closeup views of this handsome building. Below, the tracks leading back into the stub-platform station. (BALL)

It could be said that the glorious age of the railroad station started in 1830, when America's first large one—Mount Clare Station in Baltimore—was completed. A more important date might be 1871, when Commodore Cornelius Vanderbilt's red brick, iron, and slate monument, Grand Central Depot—predecessor to Grand Central Terminal—was opened in New York City. Not to be outdone, Pennsy shortly opened its Philadelphia Broad Street Station, whose train shed spanned three hundred feet, more than twice the diameter of the dome of Saint Peter's in Rome! For a fleeting moment, it was the world's largest station. Then, in 1894, the Union Station in St. Louis was completed to claim the title. Engineer E. D. Cameron designed its enormous shed and architect Theodore C. Link planned the massive Romanesque exterior and fanciful tower.

At right: the Germanic-looking Union Station as viewed from Carl Milles's operatic fountain. Below, Missouri Pacific's diesel-powered *Colorado Eagle* departs from the station's enormous shed. Opposite—and only because it's time for a train!—New York Central's haughty Hudson No. 5393 stomps into town with the *Southwestern Limited*. (FRISCO, MISSOURI PACIFIC, PLUMMER)

On October 30, 1914, Kansas City Union Station was opened—acclaimed as "the most luxurious and most modern station ever built." The structure, described by its architect, Jarvis Hunt, as "modern French Renaissance," was the third largest station in America. The frontage is a third of a mile long; the main building is 160 feet wide by 500 feet long, with a ceiling 90 feet high. The exterior is Bedford limestone and New England granite, and walls in the main lobby are of Kasota marble. The station faces south, away from the business district, with all tracks approaching the station well below street level. During the war, the station was thronged with soldiers leaving on trains that would start them on their way to England,

France, Normandy, Africa, Guam, Wake. Trains marched out amid tears and brass bands; within months, some of these same soldiers returned to Union—on crutches, in wheelchairs, in coffins. A new President, from nearby Independence, would also come and go from Union Station.

Above: the imposing station as seen from Liberty Memorial Park. Opposite, above, nighttime finds both sections of Santa Fe's *Grand Canyon Limited* ready to depart Union Station. Streamlined 4-6-4 No. 3460 will depart for Lawrence and Topeka on the southern section; the diesels will follow on the northern section. Opposite, below, Missouri Pacific's eastbound *Colorado Eagle,* seen from the Main Street overpass, departs for St. Louis in misty rain. (BALL)

The story of Cleveland Union Terminal deserves a book. Brothers O. P. and M. J. Van Swerigen, prominent Cleveland realtors, envisioned a carefully laid-out downtown center, with a rapid-transit line that would bring people into the downtown area. By 1920 the project was gaining momentum, and three railroads signed an agreement with the Cleveland Union Terminals Company to undertake construction of a great railway station and a 17.1-mile double-tracked electric line to serve the terminal, keeping steam engines out. Construction commenced on January 1, 1922, under the direction of Chief Engineer H. O. Jouett. Graham, Anderson, Probst & White of Chicago, builders of Chicago's Union Station, were the architects. On June 28, 1930, the Cleveland Union Terminal was opened, its main concourse eighteen feet below street level and twenty-three feet above track level—actually a station without a building! The magnificent fifty-two-story Terminal Tower office building followed the eclectic style of office building design of the late 1920s and was the tallest edifice outside Manhattan when it opened. Opposite, Erie's *Lake Cities* departs under the CUT's 3,000-volt DC and the magnificent Terminal Tower.

On this page are examples of three quite different stone stations. Above, at left: the seventy-six-foot clock tower adorning Jersey Central's yellow brick and quarrystone station at Elizabeth, New Jersey, built in 1892. Above, right: the great dome resting upon four barrel vaults of the Union Station at Tacoma, Washington, built by station architects Reed & Stem between 1909 and 1911. Backing out of the station is Northern Pacific's train #422 from Seattle. At right, B&O's station along "the row" at Grafton, West Virginia, with its ugly and enormous quarrystone-faced walls and contrasting quoins, typical of the many nondescript railroad stations built in the late nineteenth century. (PRINT COLLECTION, BALL, HASTINGS, BALL)

In the late nineteenth century and into the early twentieth, many mission-inspired depots were built by the railroads in the South, the Southwest, and the West, replacing older, less permanent structures. Some of the more distinctive examples are pictured on this page. Below: Southern Pacific's T&NO depot at San Antonio, exhibiting touches of Italian style, with rococo ornamentation around its windows. At right: the lovely Spanish mission–inspired station at Birmingham, Alabama, completed in 1909—a beautiful composition of pavilions, domes, and towers. That little three-car train departing Birmingham is Southern's *Vulcan,* built in 1939 by St. Louis Car Company. A business car is on the rear on today's run. Opposite: Union Pacific's very restrained mission-style station at Boise, Idaho. (COLLECTION, HASTINGS, GRIFFITHS)

In the fall of 1857, banker-merchant Luther C. Challis and Topeka land dealer Cyrus Kurtz Holliday, both members of the Kansas Territorial Legislature at Lawrence, started plans to construct a railroad between Topeka and Atchison. On January 31, 1859, Colonel Holliday completed the basic charter for the Atchison & Topeka Railroad Company in his hotel room in Lawrence, and the next day he introduced the bill to the legislature. On February 11, the governor signed it into law. The railroad ultimately became part of the Atchison, Topeka & Santa Fe Railway system's operations, on October 1, 1875, and was finally purchased by the railway on February 15, 1899.

My favorite railroad station, and one that was my private world as a kid, is the Santa Fe station in Lawrence, pictured on this spread. It was built by architect W. B. Seather for the AT&SF in late 1883, with offices for the Leavenworth, Lawrence & Galveston, which later became part of the Santa Fe. Every room upstairs was finished with curly maple chair rails and wainscoting! The building itself is strongly derivative of French domestic architecture. Santa Fe's regular "daytime visitors" to Lawrence are: (opposite) the *Ranger,* blasting out of town behind the 2915; the midday *Chicagoan,* behind diesel No. 11; and (right, above) the *California Limited,* pulling into the station. Be sure to be around the depot at 5:56 this afternoon, when the beautiful *Kansas Cityan* (right) puts in her appearance, en route to Fort Worth and Dallas! (BALL)

In 1884, Charles Francis Adams, grandson of former U.S. President John Quincy Adams, took over as president of the Union Pacific. Easterner Adams asked a close friend and Harvard classmate, architect Henry Van Brunt, to design five stations for the Union Pacific. One was the Queen Anne–like station (right) in Lawrence, Kansas, completed around 1892, which had stone and pannel brick that gave an effect of half-timbering, and a small spire (later removed) on the central section. Opposite, above: the entrance to the station's waiting room, with a touch of New England in the overlight and molding.

The station was located on the apex of the 4°2.7′ curve at Lawrence and was the central spot from which to watch the great show of Union Pacific and Rock Island trains (the latter had trackage rights over the UP). The first "standard Union Pacific railroad structure" in Lawrence was the two-stall frame enginehouse erected in 1885 for servicing the power used on the Leavenworth branch. The little structure somehow survived to the end of the 1940s and well into the next decade—never catching fire from the turn-of-the-century 2-8-0's that used the house until the end of steam! (BALL)

In the mid- to late-nineteenth century, European architects often critized American architecture as not only being behind the times, but as being weak in character and unsophisticated. America, at least in utilitarian buildings like depots, stressed the appeal of order and structural logic rather than style. While America's large cities could boast ambitious permanent structures, the country stations, for the most part, were constructed of wood, which was readily available for building—and burning! Opposite: the neat, simple, and tastefully trimmed depot at Kilbourne, Illinois, along the Chicago & Illinois Midland Railroad. The train order hoops are in position with orders for both the head end and rear end, and the agent is stationed on the platform to look over the train. No need to slow the big 2-10-2 and her heavy train.

Above: one of the most unusual stations in America, the Monon station at Gosport, Indiana. This all-purpose structure, constructed of red bricks with walls two bricks thick, has a passenger waiting room, ticket office, and freight station all under one roof. In the center of the station, a large wooden wheel-hoist is mounted on the rafters for unloading freight. During the 1913 floods, the nearby White River quickly rose over its banks and the stationmaster had to make a daring escape by boat. The diesel-powered train is #5, *The Day Express,* en route from Chicago to Louisville. (HASTINGS, BENNETT)

As the nation grew, so did the railroads and the towns and villages along the line. By the 1880s little wood-frame depots had begun to dot the countryside. Most were quaint, utilitarian structures standardized by each railroad and for the most part very unimaginative. Indeed, most of the railroads' engineering departments drew up plans for "the basic depot," and, depending on its size, assigned a number (or *class*) to each variation on the basic structure. Any individuality usually came in the treatment of the trim—and, always, in the gingerbread under the eaves!

The depots represented here are examples of basic designs that display a sense of clean-lined dignity. Opposite, above: Southern's combination passenger and freight station at Leeds, Alabama, offering Western Union, Railway Express—and Jim Crow facilities. The hogger on the Ls-1 class articulated knows he's raisin' dust and has the whistle tied down goin' through town! Opposite, below, in the lingering evening light, Chicago Great Western's "doodlebug" from Chicago to Oelwein, Iowa, pauses at St. Charles, Illinois, for mail, express, and perhaps a passenger. Of interest is the trusslike bracing on the barn-red depot's overhang. Above, Southern's *Asheville Special* departs east from the tidy wood-frame depot at Ridgecrest, North Carolina, deep in the Great Smokies. At right: the place to hang around—in this case, the Mileston, Mississippi, depot on the freight-only line of the Illinois Central in the heart of cotton plantation country. (SR, LEWIS, DONAHUE, WOLCOTT)

"Railway termini . . . are our gates to the glorious and the unknown. Through them we pass out into adventure and sunshine; to them, alas, we return."—E. M. Forster

Opposite—and perhaps my favorite picture in this book—a glorious midsummer sunrise at Wilshire, Ohio, on the Nickel Plate. It is Sunday morning and the quiet almost invites a fast freight to appear and threaten to take Wilshire apart in its passing. Above, way up in Minnesota's vast Vermilion Range, one of Duluth, Mesabi & Iron Range's enormous 2-8-8-4's heads iron ore down past the rather spacious country depot at Embarrass, toward Two Harbors. At right, Nickel Plate's great Berkshire No. 753 bears down upon the iron—and on the olive-colored class 4 depot at Old Fort, Ohio. The frame structure was built around 1882 and, like so many country depots, was a standard design of the railroad's engineering department. (COOK, PICKETT, BALL)

By April 1832, the track of the Baltimore & Ohio—the nation's first railroad—had reached westward along the Potomac to Point of Rocks, Maryland. Produce from the rich farmlands of the neighborhoring Potomac valley could now travel east by rail. Twenty-seven years later, on October 17, 1859, when John Brown and his followers raided Harpers Ferry, along the B&O right-of-way, two B&O employees were among the first casualties of the Civil War. Over the next several years, the B&O was ravaged many times by the Confederate troops. After Lee's forces surrendered at Appomattox Court House on April 9, 1865, thousands of Confederate troops traveled home along the full length of the B&O to Parkersburg, West Virginia, where ninety-two steamboats carried them on to Cincinnati, Louisville, and beyond. The war was over and it was time for the B&O to get on with the task of building its railroad west.

In 1868, a new line was opened from Point of Rocks directly to Washington, D.C., eliminating the need to go westward out of Washington by way of Relay, Maryland, to the north. Point of Rocks became the hub for both the new line to the capital and the old main line, which became the bypass route around Washington. In 1871, the picturesque

Italianate stone station with its Bavarian bell tower was completed at Point of Rocks.

The neighboring railroad to the north, the Western Maryland, had an early beginning very much like B&O's; it anchored itself solidly upon the port of Baltimore and expanded westward—ultimately connecting with the B&O at Cherry Run on the Potomac. Chartered as the Baltimore, Carroll and Frederick Rail Road Company on May 27, 1852, and becoming the Western Maryland ten months later, the road pushed west to Union Bridge, Maryland, in May of 1862. Six months later, the federal government took over the railroad for five days to supply General George Meade's army during the Battle of Gettysburg.

Above, Pacific No. 202 backs her cars to the wye at Union Bridge, after coming in from Baltimore with passenger train #121. A highly detailed, heavy-handed use of Georgian style is evident in the station building, which has a tile roof quite incongruous with the over-all style. The station building and adjoining office building, connected by a canopy, were built in 1902. Opposite, above, an FA-powered freight passes Point of Rocks on the bypass, heading east; below, Q-4 class 2-8-2 No. 4490 is heading off the old main line with 150 empty hoppers. (HASTINGS)

The New Haven Railroad had plenty of colorful history! In the 1830s, the New York, Providence & Boston Railroad was operating trains from Boston to Stonington, Connecticut, where passenger boarded boats for New York. In 1848, the New Haven & New London Railroad was chartered with the aim of eliminating the boats and establishing a shoreline railroad all the way from New York to Boston, but legislative permission to bridge the Connecticut River was denied for fear of disrupting its navigation. The New London & Stonington Railroad covered the eleven miles from Groton to Stonington, but the deep, wide Connecticut and Thames rivers necessitated that the passengers—train and all—take to the ferries for the river crossings! By 1870, a younger line, the New York & New Haven Railroad—organized in 1844 by a group of Connecticut and New York bankers and chartered in 1846—had already bridged the Connecticut and had run its first train from New Haven to New York on Christmas Day, 1848. The conglomerate New York, New Haven & Hartford Railroad came into being on August 6, 1872, finally bridging the Thames River in 1889 to operate a through shoreline railroad—without boats! During the 1890s, the tremendous urban growth around New York City necessitated adding two more tracks, making a four-track main line from Woodlawn, New York, to New Haven.

The Connecticut stations on this spread are typical of the wooden saltbox stations that were built during the period when the third and fourth tracks were being laid in the 1890s. The third Stamford station (opposite, above) was opened in 1898 as an important hub for suburban trains to and from New York, as well as a connecting stop for the through trains between Boston and New York. The stone station's windows are trimmed with modest window caps, matched by an interesting follow-through over the doorways. Opposite, below: the westbound platform shed at Westport/Saugatuck, looking east. Above, top: the Noroton Heights station and an approaching Boston-bound train on track 2. At center: the Glenbrook station next to a stretch of experimental bow-arch catenary, with the *Springfield Express* flashing by behind a "Tiger" motor. At right, during a midday lull, a solitary passenger waits on Stamford's westbound platform for an express train to New York. The MU car behind him is the last car of a three-car local to New York, which will depart from the fifth and stub-end track west of the station. (BALL)

A total of 203 railroads were ultimately incorporated into the single New York, New Haven & Hartford Railroad system. The railroad stations, of course, reflected changes as the railroad grew. Four of the better-known New Haven stations are pictured on this spread, two on its Shore Line to Boston, one on the Waterbury Line, and one on the Berkshire Line.

Above: the picturesque board-and-batten-style wooden station at Canaan, Connecticut, with its interesting tower denoting some Italian influence. This station was built in 1872 at the busy junction of the New Haven's Berkshire Line and the Central New England's Hartford-to-Poughkeepsie route. In 1908, thirty-six passenger trains rattled over the busy diamond *each day!*

At right: a closeup of architect Cass Gilbert's station in New Haven showing the building's simple archways and fine brick treatment. When built in 1923, this very classical station represented a new approach to functional design—the building, in effect, was a large room without ornamentation. (BALL)

At right is the headhouse of the 1909 Waterbury station, designed by McKim, Mead & White; it's very similar to the New Haven station except for the superimposed clock tower patterned after the Palazzo Vecchio in Florence. Below, passengers wait on the elevated platform of Bridgeport's station for a westbound express to New York. The granite and brick station, designed by Warren H. Briggs, was completed in 1905. Its entrance, ticket office, baggage room, and restaurant were all on the street level, with offices on the second and third floors. The most distinctive features of this station are the red slate roof and open tower. (BALL)

Heritage-conscious Boston & Maine saw to it that the White River Junction, Vermont, station was built in Georgian revival style to echo the architecture of nearby Dartmouth College. The classical station was built in 1937 and was shared by the B&M and the Central Vermont. At left is a closeup showing the Bulfinch-inspired cupola, with a replica of a B&M P-2 Pacific on the weather vane. Above, the pioneer three-car *Flying Yankee* (now renamed *Cheshire*), built in 1935, will shortly leave for Boston, down the Connecticut River Division via Keene, New Hampshire. All seats are reserved on this train and buffet service is available. During the war, White River Junction was one of the busiest rail hubs in New England because Canada's two railroads, the Canadian Pacific and the Canadian National, interchange with the Boston & Maine and the Central Vermont—courtesy of trackage rights over the rails of the American carriers.

Opposite, below, homebound troops from the separation center at Camp Edwards, Massachusetts, are unloaded from an extra (running as second #211) in front of the venerable brick depot at Lyndonville, Vermont. Opposite, above: a closeup of the stonework of this 1867 station, which was once the headquarters for B&M's predecessor, the Connecticut & Passumpsic Railroad. The simple, domestic-scaled building has a Vermont slate roof, naturally. (HASTINGS)

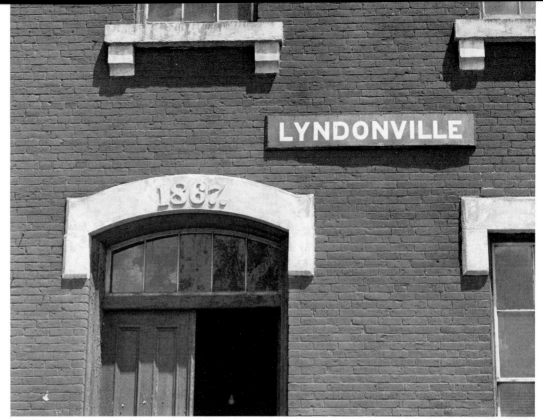

Nowhere in America is the charm and tempo of earlier days more evident than in New England. On this page are three scenes of stations—and railroading—that mirror the contrasts and harmonies of a prosperous New England that shipped her goods over steel rails to the ships that sailed from her shores. At right, in twilight, Boston & Maine's *Day White Mountains Express* approaches the stick-style wooden depot at Bradford, Vermont, behind a drifting 4-6-2. A bag of mail will be dropped off and trunks and milk stashed safely in the baggage car. Opposite, at the junction of the Claremont and Hillsboro routes of the Boston & Maine, activity flourishes in Contoocook, New Hampshire, as Mogul No. 1490 switches the way freight at the town depot. The view is from the 157-foot lattice-truss covered bridge that crosses the Contoocook River. Below, the great wooden-truss train shed at St. Albans, Vermont, with Central Vermont Railway's northbound *Ambassador* emerging from one of the arched brick portals. Beyond the 4-8-2, one of the station's two mansard-roofed towers stands in sharp contrast to the sculptured, almost flamboyant treatment of the brick facade. The station was built around 1852. (HASTINGS)

Out west, where people and places are "few and far," the living quarters of the station operators were often built right into the depots. There, one man could be present around the clock, available when needed. Coles 247's usually furnished the coal heat, although in many cases—as at Medical Lake, Washington, on the Central Washington branch of the Northern Pacific—there were fireplaces. This look at American railroad stations concludes with the passing of an extra west, drifting past the depot with its empty grain cars, under a wide, beautiful, cloud-filled sky. The W-2 Mikado will not stop today; everything is quiet and the order board green. (HASTINGS)

5

THE
NEW
ERA

JAPAN HAD SURRENDERED. But the U.S. war effort was not yet at an end: The millions of servicemen overseas had to be brought home, and the hundreds of thousands of noncombatant civilians had to be brought back, too. The hundreds of thousands of men and women, military and civilian, who were to take the places of those homeward-bound Americans as armies of occupation in Europe and in Asia had to be shipped out. And the export of food and supplies for the civilian populations of countries that had suffered enormous damage in the war was continuing.

The railways were showing signs of wear, and much of their rolling stock and many of their locomotives were often still preempted by the military. There was no immediate way around that difficulty. Orders were placed for new locomotives—a great many of them were still for steam engines, not diesels—but the federal War Production Board continued to keep a tight hold on the allotment of raw materials to the mills and factories, and deliveries of new engines were slow. The supply of passenger cars was dwindling, and plans to reequip the passenger-train fleets of several important railways, plans that

had been halted by the war, were taken out of desk drawers, but their fulfillment, too, was delayed.

And while railway travel continued to show the effects of the war, travelers who had grown accustomed to standing not only in the aisles but in the vestibules of day coaches on overnight journeys now began to look for something better. Accountants analyzing the books of big corporations that were spending, say, twenty million dollars a year for railway and plane tickets were pointing out to their treasurers that the federal transportation tax on a sum that large came to three million dollars a year, and that this tax money could be spent to better advantage on automobiles or even private planes for their officers.

The Army Air Force was disposing of military planes that were no longer needed, and a number of them were bought, at practically scrap prices, by the suddenly sprouting small air services that were shuttling postwar recruits to training centers on a charter basis, undercutting the fares granted to the government by the railways. The results of such charters were sometimes disastrous. For instance: A group of young men assembled at eight o'clock one morning in Brooklyn to be sworn into the Army; that afternoon they boarded a charter plane at La Guardia Airport to fly to Norfolk, Virginia, for training. The aircraft, its engines malfunctioning, came down in swampy territory some miles short of its destination and caught fire. The pilots escaped, but the recruits were suffocated by the smoke. Government investigators made several unpleasant discoveries about the manner in which the aircraft had been maintained and about the record of the pilots who had flown it. During the war, the classic way of sending recruits from the New York City region to Norfolk had been to bus them to Jersey City, put them aboard a Baltimore & Ohio train, unload them in Baltimore, march them a short distance through the streets to the pier of the Old Bay Line, and bed them down in the night steamboat to Norfolk. But the Old Bay Line went out of business after the war. For a time after that, the recruits were sent out of Pennsylvania Station in the *Mount Vernon,* an express with good connections to the South after its arrival in Washington; the recruits were served dinner, in shifts, aboard the *Mount Vernon*'s dining car. This safe and reasonable arrangement of moving recruits came to an end when the Pennsy withdrew the dining car from the *Mount Vernon;* the Army then had to find an alternative—with tragic results.

The Santa Fe, one of the very best friends of the railway passenger, had been enormously pleased with itself when it put into operation, not long before the United States entered the war, a train for day-coach passengers modeled after its super-comfortable nighttime train. This was *El Capitan,* which ran from Chicago to Los Angeles at the speed of the *Super-Chief,* the Santa Fe's principal limited. Because the Santa Fe's main line had—and, in the 1970s, still has—a very spacious right-of-way (unhampered by the infringements on clearances that prohibited the use of outsize passenger cars on, for instance, the Pennsy and the New York Central), *El Capitan* could be made up entirely of double-decker cars; day coaches, lounge car, dining car—everything was aboard. Passengers rode only on the top deck, and this had several benefits, including a loftier view of the countryside and a greater distance from the rails, which meant both a smoother journey and a quieter one. The Santa Fe was enormously pleased with what it had created, and so was the traveling public, for whom transportation cost was an impor-

tant consideration (*El Capitan*'s dining-car prices were deliberately kept low, and the fares were well below Pullman fare). In 1941, when the service was initiated, the Santa Fe only had on hand enough of the new double-decker cars to offer two round trips a week to Los Angeles; there was a demand for daily service from the beginning, but not until 1953, eight years after the war had ended, could the Santa Fe, hampered by wartime and postwar priorities on materials, get the extra cars needed—but by then the swing away from train travel had become strong.

The Pennsylvania's plans for new and improved rolling stock were likewise delayed. But ultimately the commodious new coaches, new dining cars, new lunch-counter cars, new parlor cars, new observation cars ordered by the Pennsy appeared and were first assigned to the *Congressional Limited* (New York–Washington) and the *Senator* (Boston–Washington). New Pennsy coaches, designed especially for overnight journeys, were coming into service—full-size coaches that had only forty-eight seats instead of seventy or eighty, which made life aboard them much more comfortable.

The New York Central and the Union Pacific were two other prime movers in the admirable drive for better trains, and there were still others. Even the Kansas City Southern, whose passenger traffic was no longer abundant, reequipped its trains with some classic examples of lightweight equipment—some of which survives to this day, in a rather bedraggled state, on the Long Island Railroad. The Burlington broke out an enormous array of fine, up-to-date rolling stock; for a time it was operating more observation cars, both parlor and sleeper, over more daily mileage, than even the New York Central, which for years had held the record.

The Union Pacific's double-deck dining cars, whose top deck of tables sat under a domed canopy of glass, were only one example of the luxury cars the railways were buying in their effort to hold on to passenger business. The Seaboard Coast Line ordered bar-lounge cars with a glass roof over half their length (these cars were single-deckers, because double-deckers would not clear the tunnel south of the station in Washington or the one under the Hudson into New York City). The Atlantic Coast Line, on the other hand, invested in lounge cars with a central platform slightly above floor level; on the platform were two rows of seats, back to back, facing outward, charabanc fashion. The Pennsylvania, seeking further to improve one of its most profitable trains, the *Congressional Limited,* ordered a set of what it called conference cars—compartments in which groups of passengers could talk together in complete seclusion during the run of three hours and thirty-five minutes between New York and Washington at the end of the business day.

The Chicago & North Western, a railway beset by the problem of competing with better-heeled railways in nearly every city of importance, nevertheless put considerable money into several squadrons of double-decker cars, some of them parlor cars, for many of its major daytime runs. It bought another squadron of lightweight sleeping cars, too. Many of these cars have vanished into history. Seekers after irony can ponder the fact that the last sleeping-car run on the North Western—Chicago to Green Bay, Wisconsin—was serviced by a pair of special heavyweight sleeping cars built to haul invalids and their attendants between Chicago and Rochester, Minnesota, the home of the Mayo Clinic. These cars had been constructed so that the outer side walls of the bedrooms could be removed; thus, stretcher cases could be put on the train and taken off with minimum inconvenience to the patients.

The experiments in providing always-better rolling stock—and the competition to do so—went on and on. The Great Northern and the Northern Pacific, which hauled the Burlington's long-distance trains west of Minneapolis, provided their best trains with several double-decker cars—seats or sleeping accommodations on the lower level, more seats and a glass roof on the upper level. The Southern Pacific built some dome cars of its own in its Sacramento shops, and its premier trains, already among the best, were improved even further with heavy additions of the best sort of coaches, sleeping cars, dining cars, lounge cars. The *California Zephyr*—a joint venture of the Burlington, the Denver & Rio Grande, and the Western Pacific—seemed to blossom forth with domes over every second car. The New York, New Haven & Hartford burst into such a fever of reequipping that it began to win awards—for coaches, sleeping cars, parlor cars, grill cars, dining cars of distinct character indeed. The Chesapeake & Ohio and the Baltimore & Ohio, then competitors instead of husband and wife, as they later became after a gigantic merger, acquired new equipment that was equally nonconformist but likewise appealing. Even the remote Bangor & Aroostook invested in modernization.

The only major holdouts were the Lehigh Valley, which held on to its heavyweight but usable passenger cars until the service was discontinued, and the Soo Line, whose rolling stock—likewise still usable—should have been presented to a museum. But even the Soo, on its last passenger service out of Chicago, boasted lightweight Pullman sleeping cars leased from the Pennsylvania.

An equally fervent effort was made to keep the steam locomotive viable. It had been in voluminous production all during the war, and it had been exported in vast numbers. All of these exports were of standard, almost traditional design; what was needed overseas in wartime was motive power that could be turned out at once, without waiting for new designs, new jigs, new tools. Some of the patterns were a couple of decades old. No matter: the locomotives were delivered to Europe, Africa, Asia, wherever. What experimentation there was involved developing new locomotives for the domestic trade. The Chesapeake & Ohio, to cite one instance, was experimenting with engines that would burn pulverized coal; the Union Pacific had inaugurated its mighty turbines; the Pennsylvania was considering turbines and multicylindered locomotives. The National Coal Association, noting that the increasing use of diesel locomotives had the effect of reducing the demand for steam coal, was taking an interest in developments; the scientists of the Battelle Institute were wondering, too, whether the steam locomotive could not be improved upon.

But the postwar steam locomotive suffered disadvantages that were not of its own making. Many of its component parts were not made by its own builders but were bought (and some of them *had* to be bought, for they were patented devices) from the railway industrial suppliers. Superheaters, feedwater heaters—all sorts of apparatus—came not from locomotive manufacturers such as Baldwin and the American Locomotive Company (Alco) but from these suppliers. As the diesel grew in numbers, there were fewer steam locomotives to be equipped with the specialties provided by railway-supply companies, and the industry began to decline. Not very long before the Norfolk & Western, a line stubbornly addicted to the steam engine, gave in and went to the diesel, one of its officials said that since some of the specialties required were in increasingly short supply, he saw the possibility of having to set up the machinery and tools needed to produce these parts, under license from the owners of the patents. The anticipated cost of all this, and the cost of maintaining a crew of machinists who could never be used full time, had decided him that it was time to part with his favorite form of motive power.

Much subtler influences worked against the continued life of the American steam locomotive. The makers of diesel locomotives—one or two of them, at any rate—began suggesting to certain railroads that since considerable tonnage of not only diesel locomotives but of other goods produced by these manufacturers was being shipped by rail, perhaps it might not be a bad idea for the railways serving these makers' plants to put some money into buying diesels from them. The Federal Trade Commission—in theory, anyway—disapproves of entangling alliances of this kind, but careful observers could note, here and there, evidence of such alliances. A subtler influence, too, was a federal law that made it much easier to write off steam locomotives on depreciation sheets; locomotives that had barely been broken in were thereupon sent off to the scrap merchants, along with a great many older ones.

Should the postwar period be called a new era? Some of the railways—the ones that still bothered to call the traveling public's attention to the new trains and to the new comforts and pleasures they afforded—did indeed appear to believe that it *was* a new era. There were many more who believed, though, that what was now happening was not a revival but rather the continuation of the steady decline that had been halted only during the war years by the special demands of the war effort. There had been new locomotives, new passenger cars before the war—equipment which, it was hoped, would halt the downward drift. The splendid *Empire State Express* of the New York Central—the express launched on its career the day Pearl Harbor was bombed: was it a herald of the new era?—or simply an attempt to reverse a tide that was irreversible?

The 1940s, and especially the first half of the forties, was the Decade of the Trains. Never before had trains undertaken such a burden—a burden they handled without faltering; never again, it now seems likely, will they be given such a great task.

East out of Hawarden, a town in Iowa, the single track of the Chicago & North Western lies untroubled on an August morning in 1949. The last passenger train on the line has been discontinued; it presently begins its run many miles to the east. One reason must be the new highway, four lanes wide, that winds up and down the gentle hills of northern Iowa alongside the railway. August is the height of summer-vacation time in the Midwest. But a man driving east out of Hawarden at nine in the morning meets, in the time it takes to cover eighty miles, but two automobiles and a panel truck. Why is there a four-lane highway?

Three days a week, eastbound out of Saint Francis, a small town in western Kansas, a mixed train slants toward the main line of the Burlington, a half-day's run to the north. Now and then it ducks its head under one or another of the new, expansive four-lane-highway bridges. Bridges of this size and solidity cost, even in 1955, several million dollars each. Are bridges as expensive as this, built to cross a railway over which a train makes only three round trips a week, necessary?

Cut Bank is a town in Montana on the main line of the Great Northern from Chicago to Seattle. In the postwar days it still enjoyed (or passengers could have enjoyed, if they wanted to) two passenger trains a day each way—trains with the customary amenities of sleeping and dining facilities. But now, in the mid-forties, an airport has been built near town, and the Great Northern, one of the largest property-holders in Cut Bank, has been assessed $35,000 as its share of the cost. The town's railway employees, too, are not especially happy about the idea of having to help pay through their taxes for something that will undoubtedly have an unpleasant effect on the line's passenger service and their livelihoods.

When the airport is ready for business, two scheduled airlines apply to the proper federal government authority for permission to use it. An airport in this country can lead a charmed life: the land for it can be expropriated by the right of eminent domain and then taken off the tax rolls. It is always pleasant for a tax-exempt facility to compete with neighbors who are taxpayers! Western Air Lines and Canadian Pacific Air Lines are awarded the right to serve Cut Bank, and they do—for a time. And at the Great Northern station in town, it is noticeable that the number of Pullman passengers on the four daily trains is declining. Western Air and Canadian Pacific Air, presumably, are picking up some—or maybe all—of those passengers. But not enough, it appears, to satisfy the air lines, for after a while both of them make another request to the federal government authority—for permission to discontinue service to Cut Bank. The permission is granted. The airport, staffed by employees paid out of federal taxes, does not give up right away; owners of private planes become the only users of the facility for which taxpayers in general, including the railway, have provided the funds. Although the railway survives, Cut Bank is still, in the 1970s, not served by any air line. Will Alice in Wonderland please step forward and take a bow?

The decade of the 1940s was hardly as promising for the train at its end as at its beginning. In the early forties a volume of freight and passengers without precedent in the history of the American railway was moving across the land. By the end of the decade, the slow, steady decline in traffic that had begun shortly after the First World War and had been temporarily arrested during the Second World War had resumed, and it is now reasonable to wonder whether this decline will ever end. To the public, its most visible sign was the disappearance, one by one, of the passenger trains. Railways that had so frantically bought all the troop sleepers, kitchen cars, and hospital cars that the government was willing to dispose of right after the end of the war were discovering that the equipment they already owned was becoming superfluous. The huge array of new passenger cars that Pullman and Budd turned out after the war were acclaimed as the best ever, but that was not enough to prevent the erosion.

Who can apportion, on a percentage basis, the causes of the decline of the railroads?—the automobile, the tax system, the abundance of federal transportation agencies doing cutthroat work on one another's activities, the highway lobby, the railway managements. The survivors of the Decade of the Trains live mostly in other parts of the world—the passenger cars in Mexico and in Canada; the steam locomotives here and there in England and in France, and in something approaching profusion behind the Iron Curtain, where so many products of Alco and Baldwin went to help win the war and to help with rehabilitation after the war. A few have ended up as the carefully nurtured pets of nonprofit railway-preservation societies. The rest are still doing the hard work, out on the main lines, for which they were built.

An American who was overseas in a railway bat-

talion during the war is revisiting Europe in the 1970s. There is an international comradeship—sometimes intense, sometimes merely formal—among railway men that makes them welcome the world over, no matter what the ideologies they bring with them or encounter in their travels. Picture, then, this American on tour. In France, out of Perpignan on the Mediterranean coast, he has waited all day at the railway station trying to discover whether one of the last Schenectady 4-8-2's still in steam anywhere in France will be required to work that day. The afternoon express west to Port Bou and the Spanish border is so heavy that a second section is required, and a Schenectady 4-8-2 is rostered for it. The American rides behind it to the border.

In Yugoslavia, he finds many American steam locomotives whose tenders cheerfully proclaim the fact that these engines are donations from the United States. In Poland, at a junction some fifty miles north of Poznan, he is escorted to a roundhouse the likes of which he has thought he would never see again—a huge, smoking crater in which seventy steam locomotives are in various stages of readiness, all in steam. The foreman, a stalwart man wearing decorations that prove his fervor in resisting the Nazis, speaks English with a Brooklyn accent—he lived in Brooklyn for some years before he came back home to stay. Over forty of his engines are Alco or Baldwin, and—like the others in the roundhouse—they are maintained in a state of cleanliness and repair that astounds the American. Poland, still recovering from the war, needs every possible piece of motive power, he is told; nothing goes to the scrap heap until it has become completely uneconomic. In his enthusiasm for his giant charges, the foreman orders three or four of his prize steeds run out of the roundhouse and onto the turntable so that his American guest can admire them.

"You don't use steam engines anymore in the United States?" he asks the visitor. "Is that really true?" He smiles when he receives an affirmative answer. "We build locomotives over here again. We sold some steam engines to India two years ago."

The American, who has ridden the footplate of one of these Polish engines on the *Taj Express,* en route to Agra, tells the foreman so.

The foreman smiles again, then says, "Baldwin, Alco—they built the best locomotives I have ever handled. They were built to last a hundred years. Why didn't they?"

The American says he wishes he knew.

On March 10, 1945, while American, British, and French armies were crossing the Rhine and storming across Germany, an impressive ceremony was taking place at American Locomotive in Schenectady, New York, celebrating the completion of a new giant steam locomotive—No. 6000—for the New York Central. Before a thousand guests and plant workers, the shiny locomotive steamed slowly out of the erecting hall, making its stately entry while sounding its whistle lustily for the first time. Governor Thomas E. Dewey spoke from a reviewing stand draped with the flags of the Allies: "I am happy to congratulate all who had a part in designing and building this new mechanical giant, the first of a series which, because of its great power, we are designating the Niagara." Dewey continued: "One of the tests of the crackup of a nation is what happens to its railroads, and when you see the stories of the wrecks on the German lines you know the beginning of the end is not too far away. We find here in Schenectady that instead of having deterioration, we are today dedicating the greatest engine ever produced for the New York Central and that, I may say, is the symbol of the fact that America is marching toward victory while our enemies are slowly falling to pieces." On May 7, Germany surrendered.

Sixty-three thousand man-hours went into building the 448-ton No. 6000, and twenty-six additional Niagaras shortly followed. Above, the second Niagara, No. 6001, slams past Berea, Ohio, with the westbound *Iroquois*; opposite, above, this same locomotive is seen in a publicity stunt on October 16, 1945—four lasses pull the new locomotive at Harmon, New York, to demonstrate the easy rolling qualities of the Timken roller bearings. Pathé Newsreel's motion picture of the event was shown in over eleven thousand movie theaters! At right, the 6015 exerts her 6,000-plus horsepower to move the *Knickerbocker* down the Hudson past Bannerman's Arsenal. Opposite, below, the stainless-steel *Empire State Express* follows the rushing 6018 west, out of Rochester, New York. (COOK, NOWAK, NOWAK, NOWAK)

The Second World War formally ended on September 2, 1945, aboard the battleship *Missouri* in Tokyo Bay, with Mamoru Shigemitsu, Japan's foreign minister, signing the surrender documents. General Douglas MacArthur, Allied Supreme Commander, closed the proceedings as four hundred B-29's droned over and fifteen hundred carrier planes made a mast-high flyby to close out an era.

On the home front, vast technological changes would take place and America would see the emergence of TV, outdoor neon, Kaiser-Frazers, electric clothes driers, among other things. As for the railroads, perhaps a *Washington Post* article from August 1947 tells the story best:

The decline of the steam locomotive on American railroads is now in full swing. As of July 1, only 63 steam locomotives and one electric locomotive had been delivered this year, as compared with 354 diesels. On the same date, 765 Diesel locomotives were on order, whereas railroads had contracted for only 24 new steam and five new electric units.

The most widely accepted passenger diesels were those of General Motors' Electro Motive Division—better known as EMD. Here, we see the smooth departures of three EMD-powered flyers out of Chicago. Above: Santa Fe's 9:30 A.M. train, the *Kansas Cityan,* behind E-3A No. 11, a B-unit mate, and Alco DL-110 B-unit 50A. At right, Rock Island's beautiful crimson, maroon, and silver E-8 and E-7 combo have departed Chicago at 8:15 P.M. and begin their long trip to Tucumcari, New Mexico, and a California connection with Southern Pacific. Opposite, it's 3:01 P.M. and two bright yellow Chicago & North Western E-7's thread their way out of North Western Station with the smart *Twin Cities "400."* (COLLECTION, KERRIGAN, KERRIGAN)

In June of 1946, a somber black two-unit diesel appeared on Lehigh Valley's westbound *Black Diamond*. The locomotive was numbered 51 and bore a small Alco herald on its flat nose. A black instrument-car was coupled on to the diesels, ahead of the train. Little else was known about the units, or the run on the Valley. After the brief testing, Alco cranked up its PR machine, claiming that their new three-unit, 6,000-horsepower diesel would "deliver more passenger or ton miles at higher speeds and at lower cost than any other heavy-duty locomotive on the rails." Confidence, to say the least! Designated the *6000,* Alco further claimed that the diesel was "designed to operate one million miles, or approximately three years, without major overhaul."

In September 1946, Santa Fe took delivery of No. 51—which was celebrated as Alco's seventy-five-thousandth locomotive. No one missed the black paint!

Opposite, below, more potent than any of Alco's PR, the Santa Fe in September 1946 stages a noon-hour debut in its 18th Street Chicago yard, to show off its new Alcos—among other things—to employees and the press. In a week, the red-yellow-and-silver trio would head for California and display in L.A.'s Exposition Park.

Above, Southern Pacific's beautiful orange-red-and-black T&NO Alcos lead the eastbound *Sunset Limited*'s twelve Budd-built cars through the interlocking at Orange Junction, Texas. This handsome train was placed in service on August 20, 1950—one of the last new streamliners introduced in "the decade of the trains." Southern Pacific ordered its first three Alco PA 6,000-horsepower A-B-A sets in March 1948, for its *City of San Francisco*; the magnificent GS-series 4-8-4's would continue to hold down the road's famed *Daylight*s. At left, a pair of Alco PA's emerges from the mouth of Moffat Tunnel with Rio Grande's *Prospector*. The orange-gray-and-black diesels also head the *California Zephyr* and the *Royal George* over the Moffat route to the Queen City—Denver. (FOGG COLLECTION, BALL COLLECTION, PLUMMER, BALL)

261

In addition to the *6000*'s—or PA's, as they are better known—Alco introduced a diesel-electric freight locomotive designated the *4500*. It consisted of three or sometimes four 1,500-horsepower units, and like the No. 51 demo, the new lash-up was certainly no gay blade! This time, however, Alco got a little more daring with the paint and went to a dingy dark green with deep yellow trim. Below, the new locomotive, in a 6,000-horsepower combo, pulls a freight on the Western Maryland.

At left: black and beautiful, the FA's delivered to the Lehigh & New England! Opposite, Alco-loving Gulf, Mobile & Ohio's FA No. 710 pulls a D&H freight in North Schenectady for the company photographer. While the longer, more rakish passenger units got the attention and affection, it is my opinion that the FA's were the most handsome of all diesels. (FOGG COLLECTION)

Three more good Alco freight customers—I'm admittedly partial to Alco, and the FA—are shown on this spread: good steam customers, and now, after the war, good diesel customers.

Above, as pretty as you please, three one-month-old FA's breeze by Shore Line Junction on New Haven's main line from Boston, after receiving some minor repairs in the road's new diesel shops. First assignment for these green-and-orange freighters will be the Maybrook line, where these, with fourteen other triple-unit sisters, will bump all steam, including the pusher on the eastbound grade out of Hopewell, New York. Before embarking on the Maybrook phase of the dieselization program, a 4,500-horsepower Alco demo worked the Cedar Hill–Maybrook round-trip run from January 5 to June 12, 1946. New Haven was sold!

Opposite, above, an A-B-B-A quartet of Cornell-red Lehigh Valley FA's barrels out of Musconetcong Tunnel with symbol BNE-2 for New York. Opposite, below, Rock Island FA's roar eastward through Lawrence, Kansas, raising both smoke and dust in the process. Rock's *Rocket Freight* paint job, regal black and red with white stripes, was one of the most handsome of all freight paint schemes. (DONAHUE, FOGG, BALL)

A little more Alco obsession: Opposite, A and B units Nos. 302 and 302A team up on sixty-two fast-moving cars of black diamonds along the Reading—and along the Schuylkill River. After the war, Reading President Revelle W. Brown—also a former road foreman of engines with the B&O—guided the Reading into an ambitious rebuild program, including orders for both EMD and Alco freight diesels and company-built dual-service 4-8-4 steam locomotives. For several more years, diesels and steam worked together along the 1,300 miles of Reading rail before the decision clearly went to diesel.

The sweetheart of Alco, of course, was the RS-3 road switcher. Compact, versatile, and in an odd way resembling the boiler-to-cab arrangement of a steam locomotive, this stouthearted diesel helped quickly convince many a railroad—and Alco—that the power of the future would certainly be diesel. Above, a brace of RS-3's head through backwoods Indiana north of Greencastle with a Monon hotshot. At right, a new Alco RSC-2, essentially a twelve-wheeled RS-3, has coupled on to Union Pacific's eastbound *Los Angeles Limited* and its new three-unit Fairbanks-Morse diesel at Cajon, California, for the climb ahead. The FM's boasted 6,000 horsepower, and the additional 1,500 horsepower help from the RSC-2 was just enough; when a three-unit 4,500-h.p. EMD F-3 diesel was on the *Limited,* the road foreman of engines had to assign a formidable 4-10-2 for the help up Cajon! (BALL, FOGG COLLECTION, FOGG COLLECTION)

In 1947, diesels were hauling one-fourth of the nation's passenger trains, and, even more impressively, were doing one-third of the switching work across the land. According to the Interstate Commerce Commission, 12 percent of the freights were in the knuckled grips of diesels. By the year's end, Boston & Maine was handling 70 percent of all its traffic with diesels! And the Monon; New Haven; Gulf, Mobile & Ohio; Seaboard; Southern; Atlantic Coast Line; and Florida East Coast were each making rapid strides toward *complete* dieselization!

Right after the war, Electro Motive, the only locomotive builder that made diesels exclusively, was gearing up for postwar production, convinced that the *entire* railroad industry would someday go diesel. By December 1945, EMD was producing 100 locomotives per month, with an ever-increasing backlog; the company leased 650,000 feet of space from a nearby war plant no longer in use and production was upped to 5 units per day, for a total of 120 units per month.

From early 1946, EMD concentrated on the production of a new design called the F3—basically a "cleaned-up" version of the war-proven FT. The builders advertised that the F3 could be used as "anything from a heavy freight hauler with a top speed of 50 to 65 miles per hour, to a fast passenger locomotive with a top speed of 102." (They were right—and then some!) Month by month, EMD increased in size. In late 1946, with the payroll—and the demand for locomotives—ever increasing, 93 percent of the company's supervisors, from foremen to shift superintendents, were men who only a year or two before had been wage earners. The old way of building locomotives—assembling each in its own area on the erection floor—quickly changed to an assembly-line flow.

The F3 was gradually phased into the even more successful F7, and by the end of "our" decade the F7 was the best-selling cab unit in dieseldom!

Above—and one of the prettiest "wedge shots" I've seen on diesels—four Cotton Belt F7's drone along the Cotton Belt's iron through Gertrude, Arkansas, with the *Blue Streak* fast freight. Opposite, above, 4,500 horsepower worth of F7's rocks through the crossover onto double rail, hauling an eastbound Texas & Pacific freight at Marshall, Texas. Opposite, below: a graphic foreboding of things to come—Kansas City Southern F3's and an F7 step out of Texarkana, Texas, with hotshot 77; in the background a mighty T&P 900 urges #7 on its way, its crew seemingly bent on getting ahead of the diesels. (PLUMMER)

269

While this last section can by no means be a catalog of the new diesels that rolled onto America's railroads after the close of the war, some Fairbanks-Morse opposed-piston diesel engines must be included—they were all benefactors of the war effort.

During the war, the *entire* output of Fairbanks, Morse & Company was devoted to war production; indeed, the company was actually taken over by the Navy. The Navy very successfully employed the opposed-piston engines for marine use, where they packed more power into less space. Aware that their first railroad diesel switchers (of 1939 vintage) were still operating quite successfully at the end of the war, the company understandably turned to the railroad industry again as the prime market for their O-P engines. Combining a two-cycle design with opposed-pistons, Fairbanks-Morse was able to pack a 2,000-horsepower engine into a single unit, with plenty of space left over for a roomy cab, inspection walkways, and train-heat boilers!

The first large F-M road locomotive—styled by Raymond Loewy, assembled by GE as subcontractor—was a 6,000-horsepower A-B-A trio delivered to the Union Pacific in 1946. Opposite, below, this locomotive is shown at Athens, Ohio, on B&O's train #10, working its way west toward delivery to the Union Pacific. Another 6,000-h.p. trio was delivered to the Milwaukee Road later in the year; opposite, above, two of those F-M's slam through the Rondout, Illinois, interlocking, moving the westbound *Olympian Hiawatha* at characteristic Milwaukee speed. Below, a single F-M roars over the high-speed #90 turnouts, heading the Chicago-bound *Milwaukee 400* past Wilmette Tower. (KERRIGAN, LEWIS, COLLECTION)

At decade's end, in December 1950, the New York Central placed an order for 200 diesel units, at a total cost of $31 million. Added to the 185 units delivered earlier in the year, Central's fleet now numbered 1,255 diesels—with 1,491,100 horsepower.

One of the first proving grounds for the road diesel was Boston & Albany's Berkshire Mountain grade, where the diesels surpassed all expectations, quickly relegating the great 2-8-4's to memory. Central's B&A was one of the first major railroads to become virtually 100 percent diesel on all main-line assignments, and this was accomplished by the end of the forties. So swiftly did the diesels arrive and take over that the New York Central gave its employees a sheet entitled "New Faces in Diesel Fleet" showing the profiles of the various cab diesels and how to identify them!

On page 32 we took a look at the B&A during the war—and we noted the Beacon Park engine terminal *loaded* with steam. The scene opposite, above, is an indica-

tion of the almost unbelievable transformation that took place in just a little over five years, by 1950. Alco PA No. 4209 is marked up for the *Pacemaker*; the Baldwin DR-6-4-15 "Babyface" trio is marked for the *New England States*—both trains had been, until recently, handled by swift and powerful Mohawks and Hudsons. Look carefully, now: that unfamiliar face in the background belongs to Fairbanks-Morse's new 2,400-h.p. CPA-24-5. She's just come from a stint on Central's Big Four, handling the fast *James Whitcomb Riley* on the Cincinnati-Chicago run. Don't be surprised if you spot her leaving town on westbound tonnage—she's got more horsepower per unit, and greater weight on the driving axles (for higher tractive effort), than anything else in the yard! Opposite, below: a closeup look at the CPA-24-5. Above, the Baldwin Babyface trio moves the sleek *New England States* over the B&A—and the Berkshires—through Charlton, Massachusetts. (BALL, COLLECTION, COLLECTION)

After the war, the story of railroading was one of revitalizing train travel, or, more to the point, revitalizing public interest in train travel. The big innovation was the vista dome, conceived by C. R. Osborn, a vice-president of General Motors, and built by the Burlington in 1945 as an experiment. Railroad after railroad ordered new streamliners in their last great fling at capturing (holding on to) the public's fancy—and their patronage. The following spread offers a glimpse of some of the nation's streamliners.
(*Texas Special,* HASTINGS; *Chief,* AT & SF; *Dixie Flagler,* COLLECTION; all others, BALL)

Though all three scenes on these pages were taken in the early fifties, the three railroads pictured—the Nickel Plate, the Pennsylvania, and the B&O—continued to operate their finest steam almost to the end of that decade. Of particular interest is the fact that in 1948 EMD placed a four-unit, 6,000-horsepower F3 diesel in fast-freight service on the Nickel Plate with the objective of bumping the 2-8-4 Berkshires from the roster. The diesels ran hard and ran fast, but at the conclusion of the tests, Nickel Plate found out not only that their great 2-8-4's made better terminal-to-terminal time, but that they did so at lower cost! In 1949, ten new 2-8-4 Berks were ordered. Above, with incredible dispatch, one of these great machines, No. 772,

handles the *Saucer,* a hotshot, west of Lorain, Ohio.

Opposite, above: on the Pennsy, one of the most spectacular—and beautiful—steam shows I have ever seen, M1 No. 6859 and JI No. 6401 teaming up to move a westbound extra from Altoona in June 1953. The pair are seen climbing Wooster Hill in Ohio. No fewer than eight of us followed this train by auto!

B&O's magnificent EM-1's always drew top assignments, meeting the competition of diesels during the decade's postwar years. Opposite, below, No. 7609—all 953,000-plus pounds of her—roars along the St. Louis line eastward toward Cumberland with a merchandise train. (BALL)

A *few* railroads did not open their roundhouse doors to the diesels right after the war. Most notable was the great coal-hauling, coal-burning Norfolk & Western, which would have closed out our decade without allowing diesels on its property were it not for—of all people—John L. Lewis! During the coal strike in early 1950 that cut off fuel and idled N&W's steam locomotives, pressure was put on N&W brass to allow Southern's *Pelican, Birmingham Special,* and *Tennessean* to continue to operate over the 203.7 miles of N&W rails between Lynchburg, Virginia, and Bristol, using SR road diesels. The N&W fought the idea, since diesels had been forbidden on the prestrike Southern run-throughs over its track; N&W's streamlined J class 4-8-4's always did the honors. Faced with no alternative other than to cancel the three trains, N&W executives gave in; green Southern Railway road diesels rumbled over the N&W, with N&W steam men aboard to act as pilots for the Southern's diesel crews. By April, the strike was over and N&W happily got the diesels off its property!

In August 1952, the city of Roanoke opened a park with a sixteen-inch-gauge miniature amusement railroad that operated over a thousand feet of track on top of Mill Mountain. The *Jaycee Starliner,* a train patterned and painted after the N&W's *Powhatan Arrow,* was the star attraction for the kids, and was powered by an "EMD-looking" diesel that the N&W called a "children's-sized gasoline-powered locomotive." Steam stayed on the *big* railroad through town!

Some of the Norfolk & Western's magnificent steam locomotives are pictured on this spread—locomotives that, for the most part, were still overwhelming the diesel tonnage performance of other railroads at the end of the fifties. Opposite, above, a class A 2-6-6-4 is joined by a powerful Y-6b 2-8-8-2 in "the battle of Blue Ridge," getting the coal over the big hill. Opposite, below: another train on Blue Ridge, employing the same standard power combination. At right, a Y-6 negotiates the tight curve eastward out of North Fork, West Virginia, while below, one of the road's beautiful K class 4-8-2's highballs the merchandise along the well-kept roadbed out of Nottoway, Virginia.

By the end of the decade of the trains the mighty class A locomotives were turning in an average performance, based on gross ton-miles per train-hour, of roughly twice the national average load for road diesels in freight service. The J class 4-8-4 and the A's also were averaging more miles of service per locomotive per day than the diesels elsewhere. This was done, incidentally, in mountainous territory, with heavy grades and sharp curves! (BALL)

Tank town America! Going, going . . .

On one beautiful, breezy early summer day over Mississippi—and during a traffic lull along the Gulf, Mobile & Ohio—the Columbus switcher burbled out to the edge of town, to the old water tank, where men had been working for several hours, sawing away at its timber supports. A chain around the tank's supports was attached to the new Alco switcher and within a few minutes—after taut rope, 1,500 horsepower, and carefully sawed and timbered planning—the rustic fifty-year-old symbol of the past falls in a kindling of dust (opposite). Quietly, and methodically, a revolution has started on the GM&O—and on all of America's railroads. Above, the end of the line has come— and gone—for the Gulf's proud Pacifics and Mikes. Across the width and breadth of the land, the story is the same. (COLLECTION)

I made my first railroad photographs just at the end of the war, and trains soon became an obsession. On this spread are mementos of three occasions that shaped my lifelong love affair with trains.

At right is New Haven's *Queen*—the I-5 class Hudson. No. 1407 is having her fire cleaned at Maybrook, New York, toward the end of her career; the date is May 4, 1947. This treasured shot is from my first fan trip, the only one I ever made with my dad. We boarded the special train drawn by the glamour girl 4-6-4 at Danbury, made a photo stop at Whalley Lake, New York, before reaching Maybrook, where the beautiful locomotive was turned and serviced. It was the first time that a particular steam locomotive was singled out to me as a "star."

While in junior high school I discovered in *Trains* an operation called Railroad Photos (later Rail Photo Service) in Allston, Massachusetts. At their office I met veteran photographer Jack Pontin, who took me to the nearby tracks of the Boston & Albany and introduced me to the fellowship of photographing trains. He showed me some spectacular recent shots of Western Maryland steam power at work, and I realized that trips away from home were necessary to photograph many of the more scenic railroads. My first real steam safari was made down on the Western Maryland, just before the close of steam operations. The photograph above, from Rail Photo Service files, is of Western Maryland's great consolidation No. 837 heading coal toward the tidewater docks at Baltimore.

At this point in my life I was spending my summers back in Lawrence, Kansas, with my grandparents. All spare time off my summer job was spent by the Santa Fe tracks at the end of our street, or across the river at the UP depot, where I soon got to know several of the road-freight crews. One Saturday morning I arrived at the depot just as one of Union Pacific's big 4-12-2's was easing a long westbound freight up to the water plug. No. 9043, a regular visitor, was the engine, and the crew was one I had recently photographed. The engineer recognized me and beckoned me to come up in the cab. I've always remembered his words: "You love these things, so it won't hurt you none to know something about 'em." He invited me to ride westward over to the Topeka coal chute. (This first cab ride was like a shot of railroad blood that would never get out of my system!)

The engineer grabbed the whistle cord and 9043's high-pitched Nathan chime cried out. Two hands were needed to ease the throttle open, and we were under way. My heart was pounding. Here I was, not just watching from the ground, but leaving town on the business end. How I wanted someone to recognize me: "There goes Charles Arnold's grandson!" On the curve out of Lawrence, I looked back past the round side of our big Vanderbilt tank at the endless procession of orange PFE reefers hanging on under our high canopy of smoke. Before long, the wind through the cab was like a hurricane; the roar from the stack was furious, the racket of whirling, pounding parts blending as the great machine settled to her stride. The fireman yelled something about the engine "kinda bein' akin to the human soul." He didn't have to explain.

```
                                        K C    7-24

C&E  X9043  JC

No 40 on time
148 called Lv Topeka 10AM
114 east    "    "  1030AM
5049 east   "    "  1150AM
9061 east Mysville 1130AM

RI #95 Dsl 70 called Lv KC 1015 AM
277 called Lv KC 1020AM  Hot train
9079 called Lv KC 1030AM
RI #91 estimated called 1145 AM



                                        CAS

                                            1015A
```

The trip to Topeka ended all too soon. Many more cab rides would come, but this first one will always be the most meaningful to me. To this day I have saved the lineup handed up to the crew, and it is reproduced here. In the photograph above, made on September 5, 1953, sister engine No. 9504 pounds along west of Lawrence, headed for Topeka. Although I did not know it at the time, this would be the last 4-12-2 I would ever see through Lawrence. All of the "Nines" were being moved up on the Nebraska Division to finish out their service, and within a few months, all freight service on the Kansas Division would be dieselized. (RAIL PHOTO SERVICE, BALL, BALL)

It's hard to end this look at the historic decade of 1940–1950 appropriately, with just one spread and one subject. After all, within the short span of ten years the railroads met the extraordinary demands of a terrible war, breaking all traffic records; Pennsy, C&O, and N&W built huge, powerful (if unsuccessful) steam turbines; Great Northern took delivery of the world's largest electric locomotive; hundreds of new streamliners appeared on the rails—many featuring glass-topped vista domes; multimillion-dollar track relocation projects, modern signaling, and welded rail changed operations over thousands of miles of railroad. From diesels to electronic yards and lightweight experimental trains, change touched everything.

But since I must choose, my nominees for closing this chapter of railroad history are on this and the following spread: the Budd Company's humpbacked, stainless-steel RDC rail diesel car, and Electro Motive's versatile GP-7 dual-service road switcher. With the RDC, noncustomized bidirectional trains of self-propelled cars (each had an engine on its roof) were available for the first time. The RDC offered low-cost flexibility both in main-line service and on the branch lines, with an unbelievably low average operating cost of less than seventy-two cents a mile. Perhaps more importantly, these cars offered a glimmer of hope for attracting riders back to the rails—the number of passengers had been decreasing steadily since the end of the war. Opposite, Chesapeake & Ohio's train #48 departs Lee Hall, Virginia, on its nocturnal run from Richmond to Newport News. Below, B&O's midday *Speedliner* (as that road dubbed its RDC's), train #566, hurries out of Pittsburgh en route to McKeesport. (BALL)

Opposite—a scene symbolic of the coming decade—
three freshly delivered Western Maryland GP-7's head
empties back to the mines through Fairmont, West Virginia, as
B&O's steam switcher chugs off the scene. In a short time—like
the coal-hauling, coal-burning steam locomotives the GP-7's replaced on the Western Maryland—that steam switcher will be
gone. In EMD's ads, the GP-7 was proclaimed as *the locomotive
designed for mixed service in yard duty and line assignments*";
at Fairmont this summer evening, half of EMD's objectives have
been realized. (GALLAGHER)